Accountability in the Classroom

Accountability in the Classroom

Using Social-Emotional Learning to Guide School Improvement

Renee Carr

ROWMAN & LITTLEFIELD
Lanham • Boulder • New York • London

Published by Rowman & Littlefield
An imprint of The Rowman & Littlefield Publishing Group, Inc.
4501 Forbes Boulevard, Suite 200, Lanham, Maryland 20706
www.rowman.com

6 Tinworth Street, London SE11 5AL, United Kingdom

Copyright © 2021 by Renee Carr

All rights reserved. No part of this book may be reproduced in any form or by any electronic or mechanical means, including information storage and retrieval systems, without written permission from the publisher, except by a reviewer who may quote passages in a review.

British Library Cataloguing in Publication Information Available

Library of Congress Control Number: 2020948891

ISBN 9781475858709 (cloth) | ISBN 9781475858716 (pbk.) | ISBN 9781475858723 (epub)

For my daughter Zoe—
may we develop our social-emotional skills together

Contents

Foreword		xi
Preface		xv
Acknowledgments		xvii
1	The Need for Social-Emotional Learning and Accountability in Schools	1
	History of SEL in School Accountability	1
	SEL in School Accountability: Exploring Arguments in Favor and Against	6
	Understanding Stakeholder Views and Experiences with SEL	7
	Questions for Teachers	12
	Questions for School Leaders	13
	Additional Resource	13
	Definition of Key Terms	13
2	SEL Approaches in Schools	17
	Background on Nonacademic Factors in K-12 Education	18
	The Effects of School Size on Academic Performance and School Climate	22
	Emerging SEL Programs and Their Effects on Academic Performance	23
	Approaches to Measuring SEL in Individuals	28
	The Use of District and School Data	29

	Questions for Teachers	32
	Questions for School Leaders	32
	Additional Resource	32
3	Review of National and State SEL Standards and Assessments in 2020	35
	History of National Affiliated SEL Standards	35
	Status of State SEL Standards	36
	Other States Using SEL Tools	45
	Purpose of State Standards	48
	Questions for Teachers	49
	Questions for School Leaders	49
	Additional Resource	50
4	Arguments against SEL Assessments in School Accountability	53
	Concerns about the Inclusion of SEL in School Accountability	53
	Evidence Supporting Inclusion of SEL Assessments in School Accountability	56
	SEL Attributes in College and Workplace Success	58
	The Perspectives of School Principals and Educators in School Accountability	60
	School Reform Success Standards	64
	Overview of SEL's Role in School Accountability	65
	Questions for Teachers	67
	Questions for School Leaders	67
	Additional Resource	68
5	The Use of SEL in the Classroom and Lessons for School Accountability	73
	The Current State of SEL Instruction	74
	Recommendations for School Leaders	77
	Questions for Teachers	80
	Questions for School Leaders	80
	Additional Resources	80
6	SEL Assessments for the Purposes of School Accountability	83
	The Purpose of Accountability Offices	83

	Matching the Development of SEL Assessments to the Needs of Accountability	84
	How Can School Leaders Improve SEL Engagement with All Staff?	86
	Effective Approach to SEL Training for Educators	89
	Helping Educators to View SEL Data as Important	93
	The Need for SEL	98
	Questions for Teachers	99
	Questions for School Leaders	99
	Additional Resource	99
7	SEL's Ability to Bridge the Learning Gap	101
	Most Effective SEL Training for Educators	102
	The Engagement of a Variety of Learners	108
	Questions for Teachers to Consider	110
	Questions for School Leaders to Consider	110
	Additional Resource	111
8	Strategies on Creating an SEL Environment in World Languages	113
	Communication with World Language Students	114
	Review Is Essential for Success	116
	Seek Feedback from Students	116
	Increase Student Engagement	117
	Making Connections across Cultures	118
	Connecting the Language with Culture and SEL	119
	Questioning and Discussion Techniques	119
	Questions for Educators	121
	Questions for School Leaders	121
	Additional Resource	122
9	Language and Culture's Effects on SEL in the United States	123
	The Need for Intercultural Sensitivity in the Classroom	123
	How SEL Situates Itself across Cultures	126
	Questions for Educators	132
	Questions for School Leaders	132
	Additional Resource	132

10	SEL and Distance Learning	135
	SEL Distance Learning Resources	135
	Personal Experience with Distance Learning and the Need for SEL	136
	Questions for Teachers	139
	Questions for School Leaders	139
	Additional Resource	139
References		141
Index		149
About the Author		151

Foreword

I am excited to write this foreword, not only because has Renee Carr been a good friend and colleague over the years, but also because I believe in the value of fostering social-emotional learning (**SEL**) within educational institutions. I believe it is important to provide our students with skills that encourage adaptability, flexible thinking, empathy, and the ability to self-calm. Through providing students the opportunity to bolster skills that promote resilience, I believe we are better preparing the next generation of students to bounce back from the challenges that are present within our evolving world.

Carr and I grew up in the same small town in Washington State. While we were a few years apart in school, I always admired Carr's interest in learning and learning styles. Throughout the years I witnessed her interests shift to include other skills beyond academics, which are currently being targeted in schools.

I fondly remember Carr sharing her ambition to pursue education and to learn about other types of intelligence, beyond those captured purely by traditional academics. Fast forward ten years, I had just begun my Doctorate of Clinical Psychology program, and she was nearing the end of her Doctorate of Education program, when Carr introduced me to the concept of **SEL**. I was intrigued by this topic.

In my own professional and personal experiences, I reflect on many experiences which together have formed my social-emotional intelligence, and I now recognize this as a privilege afforded to me as a result of my upbringing. It is imperative to find a way to broadly disseminate **SEL** across classrooms for equitable access for all our future highly productive citizens. This introduction to **SEL** also inspired me to pursue the broad topic of resilience within psychology and how skills can be taught and practiced for increasing one's ability to bounce back from challenges. I believe that through **SEL**, we can provide a more holistic learning environment to develop well-rounded K-12 students.

Carr pulls from her academic and personal experiences to deliver *Accountability in the Classroom: Using Social-Emotional Learning to Guide School Improvement.* This book guides the reader through the benefits of and the need for **SEL**. Further, this book provides an outline for **SEL** implementation while also cautioning the reader that **SEL** will be difficult to standardize across classrooms given differing student needs. Readers walk away with an understanding of the benefits of **SEL** and an awareness that an implementation plan and ways to enforce such a plan will be needed.

Those of us who work in or in tandem with this field may all agree that our exposure to informal **SEL** is crucial to our ability to successfully bounce back from setbacks and to navigate both professional and personal experiences; however, how to implement **SEL** in a standardized and systematic manner will need to be addressed. Further, while studies support that both academic and socio-emotional functioning are positively impacted through **SEL**, future research will need to address how **SEL** may need to be adapted to address the needs of special education services, communities with fewer resources, and to reflect cultural differences.

In light of the current COVID-19 pandemic, finding ways to implement pieces of **SEL** within instructional practices, while balancing support for our teachers, administrators, and community as a whole will be difficult. Public health crises, such as pandemics, are often accompanied with uncertainty and distress, which are additional traumas that impact our students. Subsequently, with isolation and stay-at-home orders adopted across states, children and the educational community are at an even greater risk to be impacted negatively. Virtual education allows classrooms to stay connected; however, the human experience of face-to-face interaction and practice of innate **SEL** skills has been largely eliminated.

Within the context of the current pandemic, I am actively involved in implementing resilience and self-care training for educators across the rural Midwest. These skills, which Carr describes in her book, are integral to fostering broader resilience, especially within the classroom. Given the uncertainty of our current world, we will all need to work together as a unified team, across disciplines, to support each other, our learners, and our educational community.

I hope this book will be a primer that introduces and advances teachers, principals, and the educational community's knowledge of **SEL**. Carr lays the foundation that sets the stage for how to integrate **SEL** skills into the classroom, which not only benefit our students but also ourselves and our collective humanity.

Stephanie E. Punt, M.A.
Doctoral candidate, University of Kansas

Preface

The name *Accountability in the Classroom* is the main title of this work because it focuses on how accountability may occur through everyday instruction. Social-emotional learning should be more present in the classroom at all levels including at **high school**. The concept behind this work came from my dissertation topic.

For my dissertation, I conducted a case study of two schools in California which were a part of the California Office to Reform Education pilot program for including social-emotional learning assessments in **school accountability**. I spoke with administrators and teachers there, and even though many agreed that social-emotional learning had a place in schools, they were not certain as to how it could best be used in accountability. Although those pieces are not mentioned in this work, they did help guide this book.

My hope is that the information presented here will help educators, administrators, and policymakers make informed decisions on social-emotional learning and its role in **school accountability**.

Acknowledgments

First, I would like to acknowledge the hard work and dedication of my mother-in-law and father-in-law. They provided care for my daughter Zoe as I continued to be an employee, student, and mother. I gave birth to my daughter during my doctoral studies, and I cannot imagine that it would have been possible to complete my dissertation at that time without their help. Half of this book was made in reference to my dissertation.

Thank you to my supportive husband for always believing in me, even when I did not. I will have to make up all the time lost to you while conducting studies, research, and writing this book. He graciously read this book and provided insightful feedback. A notable appreciation for my brother who spent copious amounts of time editing this book. His background knowledge in education and the English language is truly remarkable. Thank you to Dr. Maryann Hasso and my father for reviewing the book before submittal. More eyes make this work stronger. I would like to acknowledge my parents for educating me and opening doors of opportunity that otherwise would not have existed. Additionally, I greatly appreciate my dear friend Stephanie Punt for her thoughtful foreword.

I would also like to acknowledge my dissertation adviser, Dr. Marian Robinson, who provided honest advice where I needed it most and always had a keen eye for detail and analysis. You have truly helped shape me into the researcher and writer that I hope to become. I would like to thank my dissertation committee members Dr. Patricia Kannapel and Dr. Matthew Shirrell.

Your feedback and dedication to reviewing my study are most appreciated. I am grateful for Dr. Abebayehu Tekleselassie and Dr. Christine Mokher, who both graciously agreed to be examiners for my dissertation, for which this work was possible. Even though everyone has large workloads, they still took the time to provide quality feedback, for which I am extremely grateful.

Chapter 1

The Need for Social-Emotional Learning and Accountability in Schools

There is a need to expand social-emotional learning (**SEL**) from extracurricular activities and homes to schools, so students effectively learn lifelong skills for success. Students necessitate **SEL** for future job potentials that do not yet exist. The question is whether or not it is possible for school systems to include **SEL** in **school accountability** systems effectively. **SEL** improves student academic achievement and behavior without discipline issues, which is a win for health purposes as well.

SEL should be addressed in schools in some way. It is more likely that **SEL** will be addressed if schools are held accountable for implementing **SEL** programs and assessments. **SEL** is necessary because it provides students the skills to handle personal and academic challenges.

HISTORY OF SEL IN SCHOOL ACCOUNTABILITY

In 1983, the National Governor's Association (NGA) report, *A Nation at Risk*, delivered a dire warning: American schools were falling behind and failing students, which the report dramatically likened to an act of war. This report sparked more than three decades of anxiety over the state of American education. In the proceeding decades, the political, academic, and social discourse has produced a vast body of proposals and counterproposals for how American education can be improved, measured, and administered. Enacted in 2001, No Child Left Behind (NCLB) was the most sweeping education law passed in nearly a half-century and introduced sweeping accountability and testing standards.

Many policymakers, educators, and education researchers have expressed serious important concerns about accountability and NCLB. Some educators experienced fatigue after NCLB implementation. Teachers concede that they were teaching to poorly designed standardized tests that have hurt educational learning and reduced curriculum to core subjects, namely reading and math.

Two-and-a-half decades of **school accountability** have narrowly focused on standardized testing; due to these testing pressures, both students and teachers have become uninterested, disengaged, and unmotivated. In turn, teachers face a disincentive to teach well, which has promoted bad behavior not only among students but also among educators. The current accountability systems in many states and districts have forgotten to consider developing productive and happy future citizens because of their traditional lack of focus on soft skills.

Under the Every Student Succeeds Act (ESSA), and its potential emphasis on **SEL**, educators are now called to develop the other side of student minds: relationships, perseverance, and well-being. These attributes were ignored or informally taught without support because it was not considered appropriate for schools to teach skills that were traditionally taught at home.

Part of the problem is that parents have been relying on extracurricular activities, which are thought to build student civic mindedness and positive social relationships and create broader thinkers, which parents cannot accomplish on their own. Affluent American **high school** students have been participating in extracurricular activities at a consistently high rate for many decades, while the participation of poor students in such activities has dropped significantly (Putnam, 2015).

Affluent parents arrange for their children's engagement in extracurricular activities, but children of disadvantaged parents do not have the opportunity or resources to participate in as many extracurricular activities. **SEL** has traditionally been a focus in elementary schools. Many **SEL** programs are geared toward K-8, which leaves **high school** scholars socially and emotionally neglected during a crucial time in their human development. Students need to gain these attributes during **high school** in preparation for their college and career readiness.

Since 2009, a shift has been underway at both the grassroots and policy levels toward nurturing previously underemphasized aspects of education development that are considered important to K-12 education. This approach was most apparent in ESSA, where school climate and culture surveys and **SEL** assessments could have a place in **school accountability**. Researchers have found that **SEL** is an important trend in education policy, and there is a need to unveil how this information is used in schools.

Commonly referred to as "soft" skills, these skills are the personal attributes that enable one to interact effectively and harmoniously with others. These "nonacademic" skills or social-emotional traits—such as motivation, perseverance, and **self-management**—are the skills that allow individual students to achieve high results on all tests and in class.

These taught skills provide students an advantage that they otherwise would not have. There is a need to understand how administrators and educators assess the inclusion of **SEL** assessments in their **school accountability** systems, which may ensure that these skills are taught.

Schools are places where educators nurture both knowledge and social competencies in future citizens. This developmental focus is critical not only to our economy but to our civic capacity. Starting in the 1980s, governors have been pushing to streamline state standards and **school accountability** systems.

While U.S. schools have been focusing on technical and knowledge-based learning over the last quarter-century, they are also increasingly paying attention to ensuring students have the social and emotional intelligence they need to be good neighbors and citizens. Some states are taking the initiative by providing tools, materials, and incentives to teach and monitor **SEL**. In the last several years, some forward-thinking states and cities have been considering how to create tools that help educators incorporate **SEL** into their curriculum and professionally develop their staff accordingly (CASEL, 2013).

National organizations have developed definitions outlining the life skills necessary for college and career readiness. The key players include such organizations as the CCSR and the Collaborative for Academic, Social, and Emotional Learning (CASEL). CASEL identifies the following **SEL** competencies: self-awareness, **self-management**, **social awareness**, relationship skills, and responsible decision-making (CASEL, 2017).

Such skills have been variously labeled as **SEL**, twenty-first-century skills, character education, whole child education, soft skills, nonacademic factors, and **noncognitive skills**. Heckman, an economist, coined the term noncognitive to describe skills that are not traditionally measured by such cognitive tests as IQ and academic tests (Heckman & Rubinstein, 2001). For consistency, these skills will all be referred to as **SEL**.

With the passage of ESSA in December 2015, states must include indicators in their **school accountability** system that measure the nonacademic characteristics of a school. Specifically, schools may adopt school quality and student success indicators for student engagement, educator engagement, access to and completion of advanced coursework, postsecondary readiness, school climate and safety, and a relevant measurement of the state's choosing (Ujifusa, 2016).

Federal legislation required state implementation for the 2017–2018 school year. Under this timeline, districts and states moved quickly to identify and implement **SEL** assessments without or with little benefit of research insights or real-world examples to inform how best to integrate **SEL** with their existing **school accountability** systems. Evidence is needed to guide these efforts to examine how **SEL** is understood and used in practice at the school level.

As a requirement of ESSA legislation, all districts and states are required to align their accountability systems with new college- and career-ready (CCR) learning standards. The process aims to emphasize meaningful learning supported by skilled and committed educators who are provided with adequate and appropriate resources (Darling-Hammond et al., 2014).

The way educators value and utilize **SEL** data is beneficial to students, families, schools, and educators themselves. Teacher views and experiences may provide important lessons for districts and states interested in expanding their information on accountability systems to include **SEL**.

Since the passage of NCLB, public schools face a dominant and persistent problem balancing the pressures of standardized testing under NCLB and teaching the life skills needed for students' current and future successes.

Schools now face a voluntary choice of incorporating **SEL** within their curriculum and/or measuring **SEL** skills within **school accountability**. **SEL** has emerged as a desired feature of **school accountability** systems as a growing body of research demonstrates its potential positive influence on academic achievement and college completion. In fact, recent research is showing positive relationships between the new assessments and higher student academic achievement (Darling-Hammond et al., 2014).

SEL is already embedded into most state standards in some way. Many standards originated from the Nation at Risk report in 1983 on the condition of America's public schools. A safe and supportive environment more readily engages educators, parents, and the community.

The inclusion of **SEL** in state standards can strengthen student understanding, the management of emotions, and self-expression for all aspects of life (Kress et al., 2004). There is an overlap with curricular standards and a teacher's goal to help students become lifelong learners, good problem solvers, and thoughtful citizens. Educators endeavor to see their students resolve conflicts with words, not weapons. Students need more content and social-emotional competence to negotiate successfully through life's challenges (Kress et al., 2004).

An initial challenge to implementing **SEL** in school centers on identifying and defining the key skills that support students' development of **SEL**. A 2012 literature review drawing on psychology and education research conducted by the University of Chicago Consortium for School Research (CCSR) identified a number of **noncognitive skills** thought important for students to cultivate.

These include grit, goal-setting, social skills, **self-efficacy**, motivation, mindsets, organization, homework completion, and study skills (Farrington et al., 2012). The prevailing interpretation is that, in addition to measuring students' content knowledge and core academic skills, grades also reflect attitudes and attributes students use that are critical for success in school and in later life.

These factors include study skills, attendance, work habits, time management, help-seeking behaviors, metacognitive strategies, and social and academic problem-solving attributes. These factors allow students to successfully manage new environments and meet new academic and social demands (Conley, 2007; Farkas, 2003; Farrington et al., 2012; Paris & Winograd, 1990).

These traits, skills, and characteristics include other aspects of conscientiousness, such as adaptability and collaboration. Although these skills develop throughout childhood, **SEL** attributes developed during adolescence have shown a significant and lasting impact on success in life (Rosen et al., 2010).

In recent years, the very definition of school readiness has undergone drastic change as some scholars have recognized and elevated the importance of **SEL** skills to the same level as traditional academic competencies. There are two sides to the argument about the inclusion of **SEL** skills in **school accountability** systems. Background knowledge on data-use illustrates which to believe.

SEL IN SCHOOL ACCOUNTABILITY: EXPLORING ARGUMENTS IN FAVOR AND AGAINST

A number of arguments are emerging to support attention to **SEL** in K-12 curriculum and accountability systems. Engagement was correlated with positive academic outcomes (Fredricks et al., 2004). These outcomes include achievement and persistence in school, which was higher in classrooms with supportive teachers and peers; challenging and authentic tasks; opportunities for decision-making; and sufficient structure.

Research found that students who received **SEL** programming within school curriculum academically outperformed their peers who did not receive **SEL** (CASEL, 2003). Educators have the opportunity to teach self-control and discipline so that students may effectively pursue their future studies and career.

Certain problems currently developing in schools include teaching to standardized tests and a lack of creativity in lesson planning as an unintended effect of narrow and punitive accountability systems on students, teachers, and school culture.

There is also a national debate among scholars and practitioners about the validity of **SEL** assessments. This issue is particularly important if schools or school systems attach rewards or penalties for poor performance at the school, teacher, or student levels. If between-school program comparisons are conducted, then considering performance tasks such as projects and presentations might be helpful in determining an appropriate measure for comparison (Duckworth & Yeager, 2015).

Similarly, noted limitations included dependence on the variables of proper administration, tailoring the assessment to the age group, and practice effects. Other researchers offer evidence that **SEL** assessment results are driven by **reference bias**, or the comparative examples respondents use to gauge personal growth or success in some areas. For instance, one study's results highlight the need for improved measurement of **SEL** skills to capitalize on their promise to be a tool to inform education practice and policy (West et al., 2014).

In addition to the controversy of including **SEL** in **school accountability** systems, a key issue is emerging around the possibility of using **SEL** as a response to the ESSA requirement for student success. The final regulations of ESSA allow states to choose their own indicators of academic progress and school quality or student success, but with an emphasis on student learning (ED, 2016). ESSA also requires that these new measures be supported by research indicating that high performance or improvement on those measures is likely to improve student learning.

Methods for informing high performance and improvement include academic performance measures, such as grade point average, credit accumulation, student achievement, student academic growth, and performance in advanced coursework (ED, 2016). For **high schools**, these measures may also include improved graduation rates, college enrollment, college persistence, college completion rates, and career success (ED, 2016).

UNDERSTANDING STAKEHOLDER VIEWS AND EXPERIENCES WITH SEL

To date, few qualitative studies consider how administrators and educators respond to the inclusion of **SEL** assessments in their **school accountability** systems, as this is a new national policy initiative. Noncognitive assessments can be beneficial because of their ability to assess student reactions to unforeseen situations, confidence, communication skills, and discipline, which determine school and workplace success (Rothstein, 2014). There is a gap in knowledge on whether **SEL** assessments should be included in **school accountability** systems. Opinion pieces centered on educator and principal perspectives on **school accountability** implementation conflict.

Many researchers state that there is not yet enough research to know whether **SEL** measures should be included in **school accountability**. They argue that we will not know until there are more measurements and more schools and districts involved. The caution with **SEL** assessments may be warranted; however, it is essential to experiment to verify what is possible, especially if federal legislation suggests that these types of assessments may have a substantial role in **school accountability** policy that correlates with student achievement.

SEL contributes to student academic achievement and should, therefore, be explicitly addressed and assessed in schools and included in **school accountability**. **SEL** usage makes it easier for educators to teach academic concepts because it provides a more positive learning environment for everyone (Goleman, 2005).

The public sector is interested in seeing these skills included because leaders believe students with these skills will attend college and find higher wage jobs to match their skills and talents. Much like the public sector, the private sector is also interested in seeing students perform well. Simply, it reflects well on everyone if students are performing better in regard to international standards and in regard to increasing a college-educated populace.

Professional organizations, especially nonprofits and foundations, are highly interested in **SEL**'s inclusion in schools. Such foundations are funding studies and evaluations to examine how **SEL** is currently evolving. Firms such as Education Analytics are exploring how **SEL** meets accountability requirements under ESSA.

Once more research is available, districts and states will become more comfortable implementing **SEL** assessments into their **school accountability** systems. The research community can inform practitioners and policymakers on how effective **SEL** assessments are in **school accountability** systems so that they may decide whether they should be implemented.

Practitioners and policymakers require this data to make the best-informed policy decisions for their school systems. It is crucial that policymakers have access to information regarding how **SEL** metrics may be used along with the possible scalability of any policy so that policymakers may justify their need when there is currently limited empirical evidence to support its inclusion.

The evidence of a positive relationship between **SEL** assessments and student academic achievement suggests that, if included in **school accountability** systems, **SEL** may enhance school capacity to better meet the needs of particular student populations.

As states consider adopting **SEL** standards and assessments and begin implementation, an understanding of school-level experiences promises useful insight. Specifically, the methods of implementing **SEL** within the curriculum and SEL's ability to improve schools should be analyzed.

Emotional intelligence theory has been widely cited in leadership literature as a core skill or mindset of successful leaders and managers that has been demonstrated to be effective in students as well in driving their own successes (Blackwell et al., 2007).

Figure 1.1, created by CASEL, depicts the components of **SEL** and how they might be taught, which ultimately influences the external components of homes and communities, schools, and classrooms.

This definition of **SEL** is the same one used by the district and pilot program. Goleman's concept has been measured with a focus on emotional competence. Goleman's framework includes both personal and social dimensions

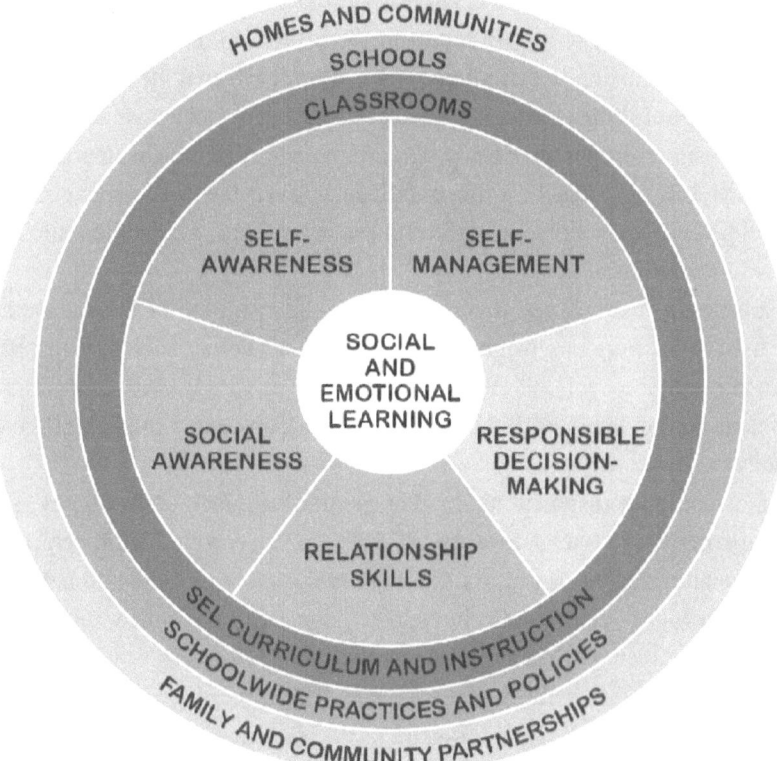

Figure 1.1 Definition of SEL and Levels of the Education System. *Source*: Reprinted from CASEL. www.casel.com. Copyright 2017 by CASEL. Reprinted with permission.

that aim to describe the focus of an individual's emotional intelligence (Goleman et al., 2002).

The key assumptions that warrant testing within the **emotional intelligence theory** include a series of behaviors (i.e., coming to class prepared, following directions) and beliefs (whether it is important to be talented or to put forth a lot of effort) that, when used together, have been validated as indicators of social-emotional skills such as **self-management** and **growth mindset**.

As **SEL** is integrated within school systems, it is expected that stakeholders and their relationships with one another may improve, which may transform schools (Clark & Clark, 2004). The process starts with a dialogue among the CORE districts to identify an appropriate approach to measuring **SEL**. Districts also consider how the inclusion of **SEL** in school curriculum and culture may support positive changes in school learning environments, which in turn may contribute positively to student academic achievement.

Districts have the ability to report on **SEL** through assessments, with the objective of inclusion in **school accountability**. **SEL** may be integrated into **school accountability** through a number of potential mechanisms: **SEL** staff professional development, **SEL** programming, and **SEL** assessments. School administrators and teachers have influence over the following contexts: school policy, curriculum, school routines, and culture, which allow the **SEL** school integration to occur.

Emotional intelligence theory supports the usage of **SEL** as a method to improve learning environments and student academic achievement. **SEL** is integrated into schools with strong **SEL** programs and assessments, which are grounded in both the **SEL** framework and **emotional intelligence theory**.

SEL-measured dispositions include **growth mindset, self-efficacy, self-management**, and **social awareness**. The objective within **high schools** is the acquisition of the necessary CCR skills for success. Goleman acknowledges that highly emotionally intelligent people can recognize, understand, and manage their own emotions. Furthermore, Goleman's five domains inform the CASEL's definition of **SEL** and, therefore, is pertinent (table 1.1).

The **SEL** data is used for administrator decision-making purposes to determine what should change within the schools to best meet student needs. **SEL** learning environments provide opportunities to reduce disruption and behavioral problems, so more academic achievement progress can occur.

Table 1.1 Five Domains in Emotional Intelligence

Domain	Definition	Illustrations of Participant Use
1. Knowing one's emotions	Self-awareness or the ability to monitor feelings from one moment to the next.	Student journaling. Students sharing college application letters with teachers.
2. Managing emotions	Handling feelings so they are appropriate.	Stress relief station created by teachers. Teachers allowing students stress relief breaks.
3. Motivating oneself	Emotional self-control through delaying gratification.	Teachers providing rewards for good student behavior. Students knowing how to complete work for better grades.
4. Recognizing emotions in others	Empathy or the ability to build on self-awareness and understand subtle social changes.	Student collaborative work. Student helping another student who does not know the answer during a presentation.
5. Handling relationships	Managing the emotions of others where they are able to interact smoothly with others.	Student speaking to teacher about difficulty with another student. Students tolerating other students who are "different."

Source: Goleman (2005).

Strong leadership is needed to instill the positive learning environment with longevity. All these components have the ability to transform schools and **school accountability** systems.

Goleman describes five components of emotional intelligence: self-awareness, self-regulation, internal motivation, empathy, and social skills, which are explicitly linked to the CASEL definition of **SEL**. The **SEL** assessments in this study align with Goleman's five components—in particular, the **SEL** assessments on **growth mindset**, **self-management**, and **social-awareness**.

Teacher and administrator perspectives on the value of these components are linked to student achievement and behavior. They should also have a voice in determining whether and how they can be taught, whether and how they can be measured, whether existing measures capture the components, and finally whether **SEL** measures should be part of accountability.

The components include how **SEL** is taught within core subjects, how **SEL** data is used for decision-making by teachers and administrators, and how **SEL** learning environments may be cultivated from strong leadership. An understanding of all these components works together to determine from educator and administrator perspectives **SEL**'s ability to transform schools and **school accountability**.

Traditionally, behavior and values have been taught at home and through clubs, extracurricular activities, churches, and sports. Although these new requirements will entail an expansion of the local curriculum and the work of implementation by administrators and teachers, it is hoped that by teaching **SEL** skills formally, student behavior, academic learning, and relationships will enhance student relationships and learning.

If schools continue to rely on activities outside the school, such as athletics and clubs, to develop these critical social skills, we will miss an opportunity to ensure all students—not just those primarily from affluent families—benefit from this personal development.

While **school accountability** changes are underway, we need to consider how they can be effectively implemented. There is a lack of knowledge on the value and role of including **SEL** assessments in **school accountability** systems at the state, district, or city level.

For instance, according to the U.S. Department of Labor, 65 percent of **high school** graduates will move into jobs that have not yet been created. The focus on **SEL** may enhance the effectiveness of educators who choose to help students attain the appropriate skills for success. This is especially true for current students who wish to perform well in their future careers, whatever they may be, as new modes and types of employment are under constant creation.

The idea of **SEL** in **school accountability** is novel and aims to meet a real need in schools by explicitly teaching educators how to create classrooms that are more social-emotionally friendly. The aim of this book is to provide information to schools about **SEL** in accountability system and the role of **SEL** in instruction and school culture.

QUESTIONS FOR TEACHERS

1. How can the inclusion of **SEL** into accountability be useful for instructional purposes at the classroom level?
2. What are some new ways to think about **SEL** practices that can benefit students on a daily basis?
3. How can **SEL** skills be used to develop students for future jobs that do not exist today?

QUESTIONS FOR SCHOOL LEADERS

1. How can results from **SEL** assessments be used to improve instructional and school practices?
2. How could the presence of **SEL** assessments in **school accountability** be a strength for your school?
3. How may administrators develop and facilitate an **SEL** environment that is effective for both teachers and students?

ADDITIONAL RESOURCE

Teaching Adolescents to Become Learners

This literature review from CCSR on noncognitive traits for adolescents is a useful guide for an affiliate term for **SEL** (Farrington et al., 2012). The term noncognitive includes other subtypes of **SEL** competencies, such as study skills and organizational skills that are not readily mentioned in the official CASEL **SEL** definition, but they are connected to **self-management**.

DEFINITION OF KEY TERMS

1. **Emotional intelligence theory**: The capacity to recognize one's own feelings and those of others and to manage emotions effectively in oneself and others (Goleman et al., 2002).
2. **Growth mindset**: The belief that one's abilities can grow with effort. Students with a growth mindset see effort as necessary for success, embrace challenges, learn from criticism, and persist in the face of setbacks (Dweck, 2006).
3. **High school**: A school that typically comprises grades 9 through 12, which is attended after elementary school and middle or junior high school.
4. **Noncognitive skills**: Noncognitive skills are any skills that are not cognitive, such as academic perseverance, academic mindsets, learning strategies, social skills, and academic behaviors (Farrington et al., 2012). Noncognitive skills include emotional maturity, empathy, interpersonal skills, and verbal and nonverbal communication.

5. **Reference bias**: The tendency of individual survey responses to be influenced by the context in which the survey is administered. The culture of a school may influence a student's frame of reference, which may cause a student to interpret a survey scale differently (Bartolino Krachman et al., 2016).
6. **School accountability**: The process of evaluating school performance on the basis of student performance measures (Loeb & Figlio, 2011). There are seven levels of accountability: (1) state; (2) school system; (3) school; (4) principal; (5) teachers; (6) parents; and (7) students (Ordu & Ordu, 2012).
7. **Self-efficacy**: The focused drive to achieve one's goals, including the ability to keep mental clarity and concentrated energy in seeking one's goals. Self-efficacy is demonstrated by controlling one's impulses and feelings to create an atmosphere of trust, comfort, and fairness (Goleman et al., 2002).
8. **Self-management**: Employees and students must be able to recognize a task, take responsibility for accomplishing it, and learn the best way to accomplish it most efficiently (Goleman et al., 2002).
9. **SEL**: The process through which children and adults acquire and effectively apply the knowledge, attitudes, and skills needed to understand and manage emotions, set and achieve positive goals, feel and show empathy for others, establish and maintain positive relationships, and make responsible decisions (CASEL, 2012).
10. **Social awareness**: The ability to take the perspective of and empathize with others from diverse backgrounds and culture; to understand social and ethical behavioral norms; and to recognize family, school, and community resources and supports (CASEL, 2012).
11. **Social desirability bias**: The tendency for individual survey responses to be influenced by social pressures (Bartolino Krachman et al., 2016).

Bartolino Krachman, Arnold, & Larocca. (2016). *Expanding the definition of student success: A case study of the CORE districts*. Retrieved from Boston, MA: http://www.transformingeducation.org/core-toolkit/.

Berryhill, Linney, & Fromewick. (2009). The effects of education accountability on teachers: Are policies too-stress provoking for their own good? *International Journal of Education Policy and Leadership, 4*(5), 1–14.

Blackwell, Trzesniewski, & Dweck. (2007). Implicit theories of intelligence predict achievement across an adolescent transition: A longitudinal study and an intervention. *Child Development, 78*(1), 246–263.

CASEL. (2003). Safe and sound: An educational leader's guide to evidence-based social and emotional learning (SEL) programs. Retrieved from http://indiana.edu/~pbisin/pdf/Safe_and_Sound.pdf.

CASEL. (2012). 2013 CASEL guide: Effective social and emotional learning programs—Preschool and elementary school edition. Retrieved from http://www.casel.org/library/2013-casel-guide.

CASEL. (2013). CASEL's collaborating districts initiative (CDI). Retrieved from http://www.casel.org/collaborating-districts/.

CASEL. (2017). What is SEL. Retrieved from http://www.casel.org/what-is-sel/.

Clark, & Clark. (2004). Principal leadership for developing and sustaining highly successful middle level schools. *Middle School Journal, 36*(2), 49–55.

Conley. (2007). *Toward a more comprehensive conception of college readiness*. Eugene, OR: Educational Policy Improvement Center.

Darling-Hammond, Wilhoit, & Pittenger. (2014). Accountability for college and career readiness: Developing a new paradigm. *Education Policy Analysis Archives, 22*, 86.

Duckworth, & Yeager. (2015). Measurement matters: Assessing personal qualities other than cognitive ability for educational purposes. *Educational Researcher, 44*(4), 237–251.

Dweck. (2006). *Mindset: The new psychology of success*. New York: Random House.

ED. (2016). *Every student succeeds act: Accountability, state plans, and data reporting: Summary of final regulations*. Washington, DC: U.S. Department of Education.

Farkas. (2003). Cognitive skills and noncognitive traits and behaviors in stratification process. *Annual Review of Psychology, 29*, 541–562.

Farrington, Roderick, Allensworth, Nagaoka, Keyes, Johnson, & Beechum. (2012). *Teaching adolescents to become learners: The role of noncognitive factors in shaping school performance—A critical literature review* (978-0-9856-8190-6). Retrieved from http://proxygw.wrlc.org/login?url=http://search.ebscohost.com/login.aspx?direct=true&db=eric&AN=ED542543&site=ehost-live.

Fredricks, Blumenfeld, & Paris. (2004). School engagement: Potential of the concept, state of the evidence. *Review of Educational Research, 74*(1), 59–109.

Goleman. (2005). *Emotional intelligence*. New York, NY: Bantam Books.

Goleman, Boyatzis, & McKee. (2002). *Primal leadership: Realizing the power of emotional intelligence*. Boston: Harvard Business School Press.

Heckman, & Rubinstein. (2001). *The importance of noncognitive skills: Lessons from GED testing program.* Paper presented at the American Economic Review.

Kress, Norris, Schoenholz, Elias, & Seigle. (2004). Bringing together educational standards and social and emotional learning: Making the case for educators. *American Journal of Education, 111*(1), 68–89. doi:10.1086/424720.

Loeb, & Figlio (Eds.). (2011). *School accountability* (Vol. 3). San Diego, CA: North Holland.

Ordu, & Ordu. (2012, Fall 2012). Seven levels of accountability for student success. *Source.* Retrieved from http://www.advanc-ed.org/source/seven-levels-accountability-student-success.

Paris, & Winograd (Eds.). (1990). *How metacognition can promote academic learning and instruction.* Hillsdale, NJ: Lawrence Erlbaum Associates.

Putnam. (2015). *Our kids: The American dream in crisis.* New York: Simon & Schuster Paperbacks.

Rosen, Glennie, Dalton, Lennon, & Bozick. (2010). No cognitive skills in the classroom: New perspectives on educational research. *RTI Press publication No. BK-0004-1009.*

Rothstein. (2014). *Accountability for noncognitive skills.* Alexandria, VA: AASA.

Ujifusa. (2016). Fact check: Does ESSA really require 'non-academic' accountability measures? *Education Week.* Retrieved from http://blogs.edweek.org/edweek/campaign-k-12/2016/03/fact_check_essa_non-academic.html.

West, Kraft, Finn, Martin, Duckworth, Gabrieli, & Gabrieli. (2014). *Promise and paradox: Measuring students' non-cognitive skills and the impact of schooling.* Retrieved from http://cepr.harvard.edu/files/cepr/files/cepr-promise-paradox.pdf.

Chapter 2

SEL Approaches in Schools

As mentioned previously in chapter 1, there are multiple **SEL**-like terms that may complicate the understanding of **SEL**. There are many benefits to **SEL** programs and various methods of approaching **SEL** assessments. Suggested methods for approaching **SEL** in schools are discussed within this section. **SEL**'s benefits range from improved behaviors, less disciplinary actions, higher student academic achievement, and increased attendance.

SEL has potential benefits and suitability for **school accountability** systems. Schools need information about **SEL** implementation; how teachers value access to **SEL** data; and how **SEL** influences school and district values, practices, relationships, and climate. First, an overview of **SEL**, the arguments for and against its usage in **school accountability** systems, and the current standing of initiatives throughout the country that are using **SEL** assessments is needed. It is clear, however, that **SEL** programming correlates with improved student academic achievement.

Emotional intelligence theory and supporting evidence related to positive internal and external behaviors suggest that strong **SEL** skills correspond with improved student academic outcomes. This finding implies that **SEL** skills should be incorporated within state standards and within **school accountability** systems. The literature proposes that **SEL** measures and assessments should be used as policy tools to inform the future direction of **SEL** within curriculum, standards, and accountability.

BACKGROUND ON NONACADEMIC FACTORS IN K-12 EDUCATION

Schools have long focused on both academics and character development, which are often distinguished as the formal versus nonformal curriculum of the school. In the age of accountability, rigorous academics have been emphasized to ensure the country can compete in the global economy. The NGA hosted the Charlottesville Education Summit in 1989 to address the need to strengthen the economy through raising standards and to create rigorous **school accountability** systems.

Likewise, the National Council on State Legislators (NCSL) passed a resolution supporting the teaching of **SEL** skills in schools (Hoffman, 2009). Shortly after in 2004, Illinois became the first state to develop specific **SEL** standards for K-12 students.

Accountability systems signal what is important to teach, measure, and monitor in our schools. Previously, only academics have been incorporated into school standards and accountability. Traditionally, accountability systems focused exclusively on bottom-line outcomes, such as standardized tests. Lessons from the decades of **school accountability** include the critique of schools' limited attention to enhancing student self-perceptions and relationships and reducing student stress.

Most recently, education leaders have experimented on how to incorporate **SEL** into school life more formally. To acquire a more holistic **school accountability** system, **SEL** must be included to serve as a counterbalance to solely academic demands. There is a long list of factors beyond content knowledge and academic skills that also influence student academic achievement. These skills are known as **SEL**, **noncognitive skills**, nonacademic factors, twenty-first-century skills, soft skills, and character. Many of these attributes have a direct positive relationship to students' concurrent school performance and future outcomes.

Noncognitive factors such as motivation, time management, and self-regulation are imperative for later-life outcomes, such as success in the workforce (Ames & Archer, 1988). Social investments in the development of these dispositions generate high returns in improved educational outcomes, including diminished disparities in school performance, educational attainment, and reduced racial/ethnic gender disparities (Jacob, 2002). These skills close the achievement gap because they teach self-discipline, motivation, and perseverance, which are key ingredients for success, especially when setbacks occur.

ESSA introduced revised accountability systems that address the evolving needs and demands placed upon schools. For instance, ESSA includes the nonacademic indicator measurement under school quality and student success, where **SEL** assessments may be integrated to meet the new requirement. States may adopt different **SEL** frameworks, however, which complicates **SEL**'s usage. Alabama, for instance, follows the framework behind character education, which is used to evaluate its educators. The term **SEL** is used there throughout. Initially, these skills were called noncognitive, and for that reason noncognitive is still sometimes referenced when discussing **SEL**.

That is not to say that **noncognitive skills** and **SEL** are used interchangeably. The distinction between **SEL** and noncognitive is described in the research. These two terms have differing frameworks and definitions. For instance, noncognitive includes categories for academic perseverance, academic mindsets, and learning strategies, which **SEL** does not include; however, they are associated with **SEL**'s components of self-awareness and **self-management**.

The emphasis of **SEL** is more closely linked to **emotional intelligence theory**, and especially the social competencies of emotional intelligence such as responsible decision-making, **social-awareness**, and relationship skills, which are needed for success across all platforms of life.

Increasingly, schools are concerned with school quality and its measurement—and which tools are used to measure it. School quality indicators in **school accountability** systems typically include dropout and retention rates at the school level. For example, the graduation dropout rate was weighted between 5 and 10 percent in Kentucky's **school accountability** system in 2000. Kentucky was one of the first states to incorporate "noncognitive" skills into their **school accountability** system, such as the graduation dropout and retention rate as an indicator of perseverance (Lyons, 2004). ESSA requires that states include at least one of the following six school quality indicators in their **school accountability** system: student engagement, educator engagement, access to and completion of advanced coursework, postsecondary readiness, school climate and safety, or an alternative indicator of the state's choosing (Ujifusa, 2016).

SEL assessments are linked to student-educator engagement. Multiple states and school districts across the country are piloting **SEL** programs. The most notable of these is California's pilot program, which also integrates **SEL** assessments into its **school accountability** system. The new pilot program's accountability system includes components in social-emotional factors and culture and climate factors, which are weighted at 40 percent (CORE, 2016).

Although **noncognitive skills** cannot be measured by the same assessments as academic skills, they can assist in academic performance. If students can acquire and improve these skills, a key task for educators and policymakers is to develop these traits in conjunction with the development of content knowledge (Farrington et al., 2012). RULER has a statistic that if **SEL** is taught, academic standardized test scores increase 10–15 percent without any modifications to academic programs.

These skills can be categorized into a wide range of traits, behaviors, and attitudes to synthesize the vast array of research on the topic. For instance, the CCSR has broken them down into five main categories using the term noncognitive: academic perseverance, academic mindsets, learning strategies, social skills, and academic behaviors (table 2.1).

These five main categories are useful for understanding the differences in definitions between **SEL** and noncognitive. Again, the **SEL** competencies encompass self-awareness, **self-management**, responsible decision-making, relationship skills, and **social awareness**. It is insightful to understand where the frameworks started in their understanding of these types of skills in relation to how they have developed.

Educators can help students develop noncognitive dispositions such as self-control and discipline, which are linked to learning strategies and academic behaviors. These skills help students avoid certain negative impulses, which may affect them in their future relationships, studies, and career. For instance, through goal-setting, self-motivation may aid in cultivating **self-efficacy** and intrinsic interest (Bandura & Schunk, 1981).

For example, teachers can verify if students are using goal trackers in their classrooms, which is a **SEL** practice. If classrooms develop positive social behavior in students, their **noncognitive skills**, particularly their social skills, will also be positive. Because poor behavior exists in schools, it is essential that this problem be addressed.

Table 2.1 Five Categories of Noncognitive Factors

Academic Perseverance	Academic Mindsets	Learning Strategies	Social Skills	Academic Behaviors
Complete even difficult assignments on time (i.e., grit, tenacity, delayed gratification, self-discipline, and self-control)	Beliefs about oneself (e.g., "I belong/do not belong, I can succeed/not succeed")	Study skills, goal-setting, strategies to remember content	Interpersonal relationships, empathy, cooperation, and responsibility	Attendance, homework completion, participation, and studying

Source: Farrington et al. (2012).

The existence of **SEL** in **school accountability** will enhance educator attention to **SEL** and provide information about their students that may guide actions to keep what works and to address what does not.

THE EFFECTS OF SCHOOL SIZE ON ACADEMIC PERFORMANCE AND SCHOOL CLIMATE

School size may have a small impact on overall academic performance and school climate. The optimal number of U.S. students for **high school** may be determined based upon the academic performance of the school (Bracey, 1998).

The findings revealed that gains among the highest achieving schools with more than 2,000 students are smaller than those for the lowest achieving schools within the optimal range of 600 to 900 students. This suggests that schools with smaller school sizes than 2,000 students experience higher student academic achievement. A disadvantage with smaller schools is typical that all students may learn the same curriculum, regardless of his or her interests, abilities, or social background (Bracey, 1998). In contrast, in larger **high schools**, students have more coursework possibilities, such as the opportunity to take four languages at six levels.

Students gained more in high socioeconomic status schools, no matter the size of the school (Bracey, 1998). The negative effects of size are far smaller for high socioeconomic schools than for low socioeconomic status schools. In another study of Alabama **high schools**, there was little quality (i.e., education level of teachers, dropout rates, teacher-student rapport) difference among schools relative to their size (Lindahl, 2012). The findings were that school size had relatively little influence on student academic performance, especially among students from lower socioeconomic status households.

School size has a potential influence on school dropout rates (Pittman & Haughwout, 1987). Researchers analyzed school data from the National Center of Educational Statistics (NCES). This data, including 744 public **high schools**, was used to test a model of the direct influence of school size on academic offerings, school climate, and dropout rate.

While school size has not been causally linked to the **high school** dropout rate, it has been associated with other characteristics that have an impact on dropout rates. Among these factors are student opportunity, level of participation, overall satisfaction with school, and the quality of the school environment (Pittman & Haughwout, 1987). In fact, larger student bodies produce a less positive social environment, less social integration, and less connection with the school (Pittman & Haughwout, 1987).

EMERGING SEL PROGRAMS AND THEIR EFFECTS ON ACADEMIC PERFORMANCE

SEL programs have various approaches to incorporating **SEL** at the school grade and subject levels. **SEL** programming fosters positive behaviors in students and improves motivation and peer relationships, enhancing the learning environment for all students. There are a wide variety of **SEL** programs that schools may implement to address a range of issues.

SEL programs for adolescents allow both adults and students to be offered a chance to gain status and admiration from people they love (Yeager, 2017). Adolescence is a time of tremendous learning—behavioral and health problems during this time which can last into adulthood. People who are bullied can become more aggressive, anxious, and depressed. The failure to complete **high school** lowers health, wealth, and happiness outcomes for the rest of the students' lives (Yeager, 2017).

Students need respectful environments to thrive. They expect more autonomy and independence in personal choices, such as choosing their friends (Yeager, 2017). They are learning to deal with new demands in school and social life while learning to deal with new and intense emotions.

SEL programs are useful to deal with these changing needs. Moreover, effective **SEL** programs can avoid unwanted pregnancies, arrests for violent crime, and **high school** dropouts (Yeager, 2017). **SEL** is economically efficient because it helps with many varying positive outcomes including higher graduation rates, higher standardized test scores, and more engagement with the community and schools. **SEL** programs capture the following attributes which motivate them to change:

1. To stand out and develop an identity,
2. To fit in and find acceptance from peers,
3. To measure up and develop competence and ways to achieve, and
4. To make commitments to particular goals, activities, and beliefs.

There are different kinds of **SEL** programs. Some believe the students need to be changed or that their skills need to be revised in some way; this is a skills model. Another perspective is that the environment needs to change. The teachers and the other adults at the school need to change the climate to be positive and supportive; this is referred to as a climate model.

SEL programs should motivate young people by addressing the values that matter most to them. These programs can try to change how young people perceive the world, which impacts their mindsets. They need opportunities for authentic voice and choice. Climate and mindset approaches include creating a mindset that harnesses the adolescent desire for status and respect. A climate that is more respectful toward adolescents is necessary for positive outcomes; consequently, a mindset that blunts the power of threats to status and respect would be the most effective.

Table 2.2 depicts **SEL** programs that have addressed topics such as substance abuse prevention, violence prevention, health promotion, and character education. Other **SEL** approaches have specific curricular and instructional components that foster safe, caring, engaging, and participatory learning environments that build student attachment to school, motivation to learn, and academic achievement (CASEL, 2013; Zins et al., 2004).

School leaders need to know the effectiveness of a range of available **SEL** programs. The efficacy of academic mindset interventions has been assessed through small-scale interventions, which are generally conducted in person and in one school at a time.

For example, Paunesku et al. (2015) delivered brief interventions targeting student **growth mindset** and sense of purpose in 1,594 students in 13 diverse **high schools** across the United States. Both interventions intended to help students persist when they experienced academic difficulty. The interventions were most beneficial for low-performing students, possibly because high-performing students had already attained these essential skills (Paunesku et al., 2015).

Although CASEL and **SEL** programs provide pertinent information about unique approaches to curriculum, they do not provide information on how educators use **SEL** data. This work discerns educators' response to their own enhanced comprehension of student growth, especially because this new information was not previously available because the **SEL** data did not exist.

Table 2.2 Available SEL Programs, 2018

SEL Program	Grade Level	Addressed SEL Skills	Lessons	Unique Approach
Caring School Community	K-6	Social skills	Forty Cross-Age Buddies activities promote bonding between pairs of older and younger students while exploring a wide range of academic subjects.	The program is organized around four core educational practices: Class Meetings, Cross-Age Buddies, Homeside Activities, and School-wide Community-Building Activities.
Competent Kids, Caring Communities	K-5	Responsible decision-making	Opening questions are designed to motivate students and focus their attention. In addition to the classroom activities, one component promotes family-school collaboration, including sessions for families.	Competent Kids, Caring Communities is designed to promote important life skills in students.
Promoting Alternative Thinking Strategies (PATHS)	Pre-K-12	Responsible decision-making, self-awareness, and self-management	Each lesson is scripted, beginning with an introduction that states background and goals, implementation guidelines, suggestions for engaging parents, a list of common questions and answers, supplementary activities (some of which connect to academics), and/or family handouts.	The PATHS program promotes peaceful conflict resolution, emotion regulation, empathy, and responsible decision-making.

(Continued)

Table 2.2 Available SEL Programs, 2018 (Continued)

SEL Program	Grade Level	Addressed SEL Skills	Lessons	Unique Approach
Positive Action	Pre-K-12	Self-management and social skills	Each grade has approximately 140 sequenced lessons, all of which include a step-by-step script organized around a different theme.	The Positive Action program is designed to promote a healthy self-concept and to establish positive actions for the body and mind. The program emphasizes effective self-management, social skills, character, and mental health, as well as skills for setting and achieving goals.
Responsive Classroom	K-6	Self-awareness, self-management, and social skills	The approach incorporates ten essential teaching practices and practical strategies, including morning meetings, rule creation, interactive modeling, positive teacher language, logical consequences, guided academic discovery, academic choice, classroom organization, collaborative problem-solving, and guidelines for working with families.	The Responsive Classroom approach is designed to create classrooms that are responsive to children's physical, emotional, social, and intellectual needs through developmentally appropriate educational experiences.

Program	Grades	Competencies	Key Features	Description
Recognizing, Understanding, Labeling, Expressing, and Regulating (RULER) Emotions Approach	K–8	Self-awareness, self-management, and social skills	The program uses four tools: the charter (classroom agreement), the mood meter (identifying emotions), the meta-moment (reflecting on emotions to change them), and the blue print (making a plan when emotions are overtaking other life goals). Each tool helps foster a healthy SEL environment.	RULER was founded on the premise that students will be more effective when they become emotionally literate, that is, they develop their RULER skills (recognize, understand, label, express, and regulate), appreciate the value of these skills, and use these skills to problem-solving and interact effectively with others.
Social Decision-Making/Problem-Solving Program	K–8	Responsible decision-making and social awareness	Sessions follow a structure that includes an introduction to the topic, modeling of the skill, opportunities for practice, reflection and discussion, and suggestions for practice beyond the structured lesson.	The Social Decision-Making/Problem-Solving Program covers approximately 30 topics each year designed to develop self-control, social awareness, and effective decision-making skills. The program contains separate sets of lessons each year.
Tribes Learning Communities	K–12	Social-awareness and social skills	Key program structures and educational practices supported by the program include cooperative learning groups (comprising three to six students) that work together throughout the entire school year and Community Circles.	The Tribes Learning Communities process includes four community strategies: attentive listening, appreciation/no put-downs, the right to pass—the right to participate, and mutual respect.

Source: Brackett et al. (2012) and CASEL (2012).

It is not sufficient to know which **SEL** programs have a general impact on student academic achievement. Teachers benefit from understanding where their students stand social-emotionally; they may use this information to redirect their lessons for more meaningful engagement, which leads to improved learning outcomes.

Positive Behavior Intervention Supports (PBIS) is a method by which **SEL** may be disseminated throughout a school system. In this proactive approach to school-wide discipline, behavioral expectations are clearly defined and taught and regularly acknowledged and rewarded (Longshore, 2016).

A misconception arises with PBIS as it is thought to replace a discipline code. Nevertheless, the rules and consequences are clearly outlined and consistently followed. There is no restriction or consequence-based strategy. PBIS adds positive and prevention strategies to an already existing disciplinary system. In addition to the school's traditional discipline, staff teach appropriate behaviors and model it themselves.

Proactive measures are taken to establish a climate where "good" behavior is the norm. Some features of PBIS include the following: (1) expectations are clearly defined; (2) appropriate behaviors are labeled in actions; (3) PBIS is explicitly taught; and (4) appropriate behaviors are acknowledged and rewarded (Longshore, 2016).

APPROACHES TO MEASURING SEL IN INDIVIDUALS

As interest in measuring nonacademic skills has grown among educators and policymakers, so has the development of assessment options to measure these unique factors (Nagaoka et al., 2015). The pilot program used both student self-report measures and teacher-report measures, both of which have potential benefits and limitations.

The data from these assessments assist principals and teachers reflect on how various types of assessment features may be accessible and useful to their schools. These assessments bring both benefits and liabilities to schools in that they permit schools to know how their students are doing in their **SEL** behaviors, but they also maintain that the schools are accountable for these very behaviors.

A Likert scale is the most common method used in self-report assessments. On such assessments, students are asked to rate their skills on a scale ranging from "strongly agree" to "strongly disagree." Generally, self-report questionnaires can be administered easily and quickly and are reliable when making comparisons within classrooms.

Research demonstrates that these questionnaires are relatively predictive of outcomes such as academic achievement, which renders them useful in helping teachers gauge student **SEL** progress as they correlate with the level of attained academic achievement (Duckworth & Yeager, 2015; Pearson, 2016).

However, self-report measures have several major limitations. First, they require high-level cognitive processing in students both to understand and answer the questions, which can be challenging for some students as it requires metacognition, an ability that will vary across students. Second, they are subject to **reference bias**, which occurs when students change their responses due to a differing standard of comparison.

A child deciding whether she is a hard worker must think of a standard measure of comparison with which she can compare her habits. For example, a student with high standards might consider a hard worker to be someone who does all of his or her homework well before bedtime. Another student might consider a hard worker to be someone who brings home assignments and attempts to complete them all but does not necessarily do so every time (West, 2014).

Finally, self-report measures reflect **social desirability bias**, such that students' responses reflect their perception of a desired response by their teachers. Across schools and classrooms, teachers and students may have different expectations for the skill levels of their students and themselves both across and within different grade levels; therefore, students with similar skill levels may report themselves differently as a result of teachers' expectations. Similarly, teachers harbor bias toward high scores, as they plan and hope for their students' scores to reflect favorably on their teaching (Duckworth & Yeager, 2015; Lombardi et al., 2011; NHDOE, u.d.).

THE USE OF DISTRICT AND SCHOOL DATA

District-centered data systems transform schools when they provide meaningful data to stakeholders that can raise questions, identify issues, and make informed decisions (Schmoker, 2008). Two main promoting factors for effective data use in schools are strong leadership and a coherent set of goals.

Prohibitive factors for a successful data system include a lack of a comprehensive data system, little to no knowledge and skills, and lack of staff support. Strong leadership along with a collaborative culture, which is set by the district and school administrators, can instill greater value on effective data use (Parke, 2012).

These preventing factors, particularly a lack of knowledge and skills, occur because the district is overwhelmed by the large amount of data, and the staff most likely have not allocated the time and resources to learn a new data system. If the district does not have the personnel to make data meaningful, they become "data rich and information poor" (Carroll & Carroll, 2002).

A very important use of data is to determine whether a new program or initiative should be promoted within schools and classrooms. A district can learn more about the data they currently have, but additional data may be needed, including surveys, interviews, or other relevant measures.

Before data work can commence, there must be an agreement on the roles and responsibilities of the data analysis participants. In one team, everyone can work on all aspects of the process. For instance, a staff member in the assessment office may extract the data, another person with statistical knowledge is selected to conduct the analysis, and administrators and teachers meet to interpret the meaning of the results (Parke, 2012).

Structures and the timeframe for conducting the analysis should be discussed before the work and interpretation occurs. If the staff does not have the skills to conduct the data analysis, outside entities may be recruited for the work. Some possible entities include local community/educational organizations and faculty and researchers at universities and other institutions.

Once the work is complete, whether it is in-house or external, the results can be presented in a plethora of ways, dependent upon the type of analysis. For teachers, it is best to present the results in an in-person group setting; however, there may not be sufficient time to host a question-and-answer session with school personnel.

Teachers may receive the results on their desk or in their mailbox with little to no opportunity to read the results carefully and question the interpretation of the findings. School staff or outside researchers should carefully format the presentation of the data analysis results to ensure it is engaging for readers. It is best to provide an opportunity to discuss the results in person in an interactive, exploratory manner.

The format of the results content should be tailored to the type of audience to which the data are directed, particularly to anyone whom the data will benefit. For several types of stakeholders, multiple reports can be disseminated. For example, a report with detailed results for each research question, which resembles the results section of a research paper, would be appropriate for the data and assessment office.

The same report with statistics removed could be created for central office administrators, which could start with an executive summary that describes the outcomes, recommendations, and implications. Finally, a separate report for teachers could include a detailed description of how the results could be useful for classroom instruction (Carroll & Carroll, 2002).

Data should drive the district and school efforts, resources, and time in a positive and meaningful way. Data can aid in identifying the most effective learning environments for the classroom where success is evident. However, there is little research on the use of data; nonetheless, most districts can use results to bolster student and school performance and change negative preconceived notions around connection to schools, student motivation, and student abilities to face conflict and challenges (Honig & Coburn, 2008).

In sum, the **SEL** term can be used almost interchangeably with other like terms, such as **noncognitive skills**, character education, whole child education, and many more. As mentioned previously at the beginning of this chapter, the main differences in terminology are because of the specific traits listed under each term. For instance, academic perseverance, academic mindsets, and learning strategies are noncognitive traits, but are not included in **SEL**.

SEL programs in particular are beneficial because of their ability to aid students overcome conflict and trauma; they allow students to perform in a positive learning environment. These programs promote tolerance and respect among both students and staff.

One method for **SEL** assessments includes self-assessment questionnaires using Likert scales, which can rate connections to schools, ability to confront challenges successfully, and their interest in collaborating with others. These assessments are vital for effective **SEL** implementation and improvements when necessary. School systems produce an overwhelming amount of data which may not always be the data they need. Surveys and interviews may be necessary to yield more relevant **SEL** data.

As a next step, a productive system to promote **SEL** in schools is through a **SEL** advisory committee, or a culture and climate team, which the school administration could encourage to conduct research, suggest lessons, and change recommendations regarding **SEL** to correlate with ongoing needs. This will be further explored in chapter 3.

QUESTIONS FOR TEACHERS

1. How could my interpretation and understanding of **SEL** influence my instruction?
2. How may I use a **SEL** program to deliver instruction constructively?
3. If available, how could I use **SEL** student data to make instructional decisions?

QUESTIONS FOR SCHOOL LEADERS

1. How could an **SEL** advisory committee or other similar team be useful at my school? What could they accomplish?
2. What types of **SEL** data from teachers and students would we need? In which form should they be: self-assessments, surveys, and/or interviews?
3. How could the **SEL** data be used at my school? What action steps could the data imply?

ADDITIONAL RESOURCE

Measurement Matters: Assessing Personal Qualities Other than Cognitive Ability for Educational Purposes

This journal article discusses confusion over terminology for **SEL** competencies. It also discusses the challenges surrounding **SEL** assessments. A discussion of the advantages and disadvantages of various measurement types is included (Duckworth & Yeager, 2015). Each assessment's imperfections are analyzed for suitability and matching with **SEL** programs and initiatives.

Ames, & Archer. (1988). Achievement goals in the classroom: Students' learning strategies and motivation processes. *Journal of Educational Psychology, 80*(3), 260–267.

Bandura, & Schunk. (1981). Cultivating competence, self-efficacy, and intrinsic interest through proximal self-motivation. *Journal of Personality and Social Psychology*, *41*, 586–598.

Bracey. (1998). An optimal size for high schools? *Phi Delta Kappan*, *79*(5), 406.

Carroll, & Carroll. (2002). *Statistics made simple for school leaders: Data-driven decision making*. Lanham, MD: ScarecrowEducation.

CASEL. (2013). CASEL's collaborating districts initiative (CDI). Retrieved from http://www.casel.org/collaborating-districts/.

CORE. (2016). The school quality improvement index & the CORE data collaborative. Retrieved from http://coredistricts.org/wp-content/uploads/2016/01/CORE-Data-Collaborative-v3-1-21-16.pdf.

Duckworth, & Yeager. (2015). Measurement matters: Assessing personal qualities other than cognitive ability for educational purposes. *Educational Researcher*, *44*(4), 237–251.

Farrington, Roderick, Allensworth, Nagaoka, Keyes, Johnson, & Beechum. (2012). *Teaching adolescents to become learners: The role of noncognitive factors in shaping school performance—A critical literature review* (978-0-9856-8190-6). Retrieved from http://proxygw.wrlc.org/login?url=http://search.ebscohost.com/login.aspx?direct=true&db=eric&AN=ED542543&site=ehost-live.

Hoffman. (2009). Reflecting on social emotional learning: A critical perspective on trends in the United States. *Review of Educational Research*, *79*(2), 533–556.

Honig, & Coburn. (2008). Evidence-based decision making in school district central offices: Toward a policy and research agenda. *Educational Policy*, *22*(4), 578–608.

Jacob. (2002). Where the boys aren't: Non-cognitive skills, returns to school and the gender gap in higher education. *Economics of Education Review*, *21*(6), 589–598.

Lindahl. (2012). A study of school size among Alabama's public high schools. *International Journal of Education Policy and Leadership*, *7*(1), 1–27.

Lombardi, Seburn, & Conley. (2011). Development and inititial validation of a measure of academic behaviors associated with college and career readiness. *Journal of Career Assessment*, *19*(4), 375–391.

Longshore. (2016). Play your cards right. *Principal Leadership*, *16*(8), 53–55.

Lyons. (2004). The influence of socioeconomic factors on Kentucky's public school accountability system: Does poverty impact school effectiveness? *Education Policy Analysis Archives*, *12*, 37.

Nagaoka, Farrington, Ehrlich, & Heath. (2015). *Foundations for young adult success: A developmental framework*. Retrieved from Chicago, IL: https://consortium.uchicago.edu/sites/default/files/publications/Wallace%20Report.pdf.

NHDOE. (u.d.). New Hampshire accountability pilot overview: Performance assessment of competency education (PACE).

Parke. (2012). Making use of district and school data. *Practical Assessment, Research & Evaluation, 17*(1), 10.

Paunesku, Walton, Romero, Smith, Yeager, & Dweck. (2015). Mindset interventions are a scalable treatment for academic underachievement. *Psychological Science, 26*(6), 784–793.

Pearson. (2016). *Measurement of student level skills: The Virginia 5 Cs.* Arlington, VA: CNA.

Pittman, & Haughwout. (1987). Influence of high school size on dropout rate. *Education Evaluation and Policy Analysis, 9*(4), 337–343.

Schmoker. (2008). Measuring what matters. *Educational Leadership, 66*(4), 70–74.

Ujifusa. (2016). Fact check: Does ESSA really require "non-academic" accountability measures? *Education Week.* Retrieved from http://blogs.edweek.org/edweek/campaign-k-12/2016/03/fact_check_essa_non-academic.html.

West. (2014). The limitation of self-report measures of non-cognitive skills. Retrieved from http://www.brookings.edu/research/papers/2014/12/18-chalkboard-non-cognitive%20west.

Yeager. (2017). Social and emotional learning programs for adolescents. *The Future of Children, 27*(1), 73–94.

Zins, Weissberg, Wang, & Walberg. (2004). *Building academic success on social and emotional learning: What does the research say?* New York, NY: Teachers College Press.

Chapter 3

Review of National and State SEL Standards and Assessments in 2020

There are state differences in characteristics for college and career success. Not all states have evidence of outcomes, but this is in the process of changing. It is the school district's discretion which **SEL** development benchmarks the state will use. **SEL** standards decide the **SEL** program a state chooses. At least ten states have decided to include **SEL** standards since 2017 because of the states' quick action to see the value of **SEL**.

HISTORY OF NATIONAL AFFILIATED SEL STANDARDS

According to the Common Core State Standards (CCSS), the English language arts (ELA) and content area literacy components have been critical to CCR in **high schools**. Under CCSS, students are required to perform rigorously academically, especially with higher-order thinking. Particularly in the early grades, there is much more attention to such matters as students' social, emotional, and physical developmental approaches to learning (Common Core State Standards, 2016).

Similar to CCSS, **SEL** is also reflected in the National Health Education Standards. Standard number 4 states, "Students will demonstrate the ability to use interpersonal communication skills to enhance health and avoid or reduce health risks." The rationale for this measure has been the following: Effective communication is known to enhance personal, family, and community health.

This standard focuses on how responsible individuals use verbal and nonverbal skills to develop and maintain healthy personal relationships.

The ability to organize and convey information and feelings is the basis for strengthening interpersonal interactions and reducing or avoiding conflict (CDC, 2016). There have been multiple indicators for all grade levels that determine the effectiveness of this standard from grades pre-K to 12. These indicators focus on conflict resolution and interpersonal relationship building through demonstration of effective and positive communication. In addition to these nationwide standards, **SEL** standards are practiced across multiple states.

STATUS OF STATE SEL STANDARDS

SEL standards currently are incorporated into state standards. State-level standards for **SEL** do not guarantee changes in practice unless they are accompanied by supports (Friedman et al., 2014).

According to a Rennie Center Report, forty-four states have not promoted **SEL** independently as a standalone set of standards, but rather have integrated **SEL** into existing standards (Friedman et al., 2014). **SEL**'s adaptability and easy compatibility with other similar frameworks were labeled "an asset," as it facilitates the inclusion of these traits within the broader educational mission (Friedman et al., 2014).

While states and the federal government have not attended to **SEL** skills as a core component of the ESSA legislation, there are promising examples that may support its expansion and replication. A number of districts have developed target strategies to advance school capacity to support **SEL** (Garcia, 2014).

Specifically, fourteen states have included **SEL** standards that are on their own, integrated with other standards for at least some grades pre-K-12, or have relevant guidelines for the purpose of this review. California is incorporating **SEL** into **school accountability** without an official set of state standards.

Illinois

Illinois has included **SEL** as preschool benchmarks. Their learning standards have eight goals including identifying and managing one's emotions and behavior and recognizing one's own uniqueness and personal qualities (ISBE, 2013). The state also has included **SEL** standards for students in grades K-12. Each standard contains five benchmark levels, which describe what students should know and be able to accomplish.

The goals include the development of self-awareness and **self-management** skills, the use of **social awareness** and interpersonal skills, and the demonstration of decision-making skills and responsible behaviors in personal, school, and community contexts (ISBE, 2016). These **SEL** standards share a commonality with the National Health Standards and are validated by the **emotional intelligence theory**, particularly under personal competency.

The standards include the following for the first goal: identify and manage one's emotions and behaviors; recognize personal qualities and external supports; and demonstrate skills related to achieving personal and academic goals. The second goal contains the following standards: recognize the feelings and perspectives of others; recognize individual and group similarities and differences; and use communication and social skills to interact effectively with others.

Lastly, the third goal focuses on the following standards: consider ethical, safety, and societal factors in making decisions; apply decision-making skills to deal responsibly with daily academic and social situations; and contribute to the well-being of one's school and community.

These ten **SEL** learning standards are specific statements of the knowledge and skills within a goal that students should know and be able to do. Each standard contains five benchmark levels (early elementary, late elementary, middle/junior high, early **high school**, and late **high school**), which describe what students should know and be able to accomplish.

The standards and benchmarks were expected to meet the following criteria: be clear and meaningful to educators, students, parents, and the community; include an appropriate combination of knowledge and skills; be specific enough to convey what students should learn, but broad enough to allow for a variety of approaches to teaching and aligning curriculum; and be specific enough to allow for classroom assessments to measure student progress (ISBE, 2016).

Performance descriptors are the most specific learning targets that build upon the standards and benchmarks. They are designed to help educators select and design curricula, classroom activities and instruction, and performance-based and other assessments aligned with the standards. Descriptors are helpful in mapping curriculum or validating what a school or district has already developed and implemented.

Illinois uses a WorkKeys job skills assessment system developed by ACT. In addition to Illinois, thirty-one other states are using WorkKeys to assess employability skills and/or applied academics (CEP, 2013). Illinois also uses National Occupational Competency Testing Institute (NOCTI) assessments to assess employability skills (CEP, 2013). Twenty-five other states use the NOCTI assessments.

Although the majority of the states are using content-based NOCTI assessments, there are more specific noncognitive skill-related NOCTI assessments offered: the twenty-first-century skills for workplace success which assesses collaboration and critical thinking (CEP, 2013).

Kansas

Kansas has adopted the "Social, Emotional, Character Development (SECD) standards" in 2012, which were designed to help safeguard children and promote their success through academic and life skills. Kansas received support from the U.S. Department of Education's Partnership in Character Education Grant Program (PCEP) and was the first state to develop such standards (KDOE, u.d.).

Kansas has made progress in setting formal priorities for **SEL** in multiple ways including the following goals (Fried et al., 2015):

- A state board mission statement that includes support for **SEL** and character development
- Designing a new school accreditation system incorporating **SEL**
- Creating a cross-stakeholder committee to align the SECD standards with other initiatives such as CCR

Under the College and Career Ready goals of the state, the students should work independently and collaboratively with efficiency and effectiveness; they should strive for excellence by committing to hard work, persistence, and internal motivation; and they should exhibit creativity and innovation, critical thinking, and effective problem-solving. Educators use a Likert scale for SECD student growth measures. **Self-efficacy** is of particular note within these standards, particularly persistence and internal motivation, which are related to **growth mindset**.

Maine

A subset of Maine's Guiding Principles, the name of Maine's standards, focuses on skills that are inherently social-emotional in nature. This subset states that a student should also be self-directed and a lifelong learner who

- recognizes the need for information and locates and evaluates resources;
- applies knowledge to set goals and make informed decisions;
- applies knowledge in new contexts;
- demonstrates initiative and independence;
- demonstrates flexibility including the ability to learn, unlearn, and relearn;
- demonstrates reliability and concern for quality; and
- uses interpersonal skills to learn and work with individuals from diverse backgrounds.

The guidelines suggest that students become integrative and informed thinkers who gain and apply knowledge across disciplines and learning context and to real-life situations with and without technology; evaluate and synthesize information from multiple sources; apply ideas across disciplines; and apply systems thinking to understand, interact, and influence (MDOE, u.d.).

These guidelines align well with **self-efficacy** within **emotional intelligence theory**, with its principle to set goals, and it aligns, specifically social competence, in its principle to use interpersonal skills.

Michigan

Most of the states' competencies in **SEL** are similar. Michigan has created three to four indicators for each **SEL** trait such as "demonstrate an awareness of their emotions" for self-awareness and "demonstrate honesty and integrity" for **self-management** (MDE, 2017). These similar traits and focuses of each state show a congruency in definitions and measurements of **SEL** and affiliate competencies.

Broken up by grade level, the state provides benchmarks of the **SEL** competencies students should master. For instance, for students grades 9–10, in the category of self-awareness, they should be able to "distinguish their real feelings from how others expect them to feel" (MDE, 2017). In grades 11 and 12, they should be able to describe how changing their interpretation of an event can alter how they feel about it.

These benchmarks are extremely effective for school systems, schools, and classroom teachers to identify the benchmarks their students should be reaching. If they are not meeting these benchmarks, they can provide the relevant **SEL** programmatic supports where they are needed.

Minnesota

This **SEL** implementation guidance is a suggested framework for comprehensive district-wide **SEL** implementation using CASEL's Theory of Action framework, which includes the following milestones (MDE, 2020).

- Develop a vision that prioritizes academic, social, and emotional learning.
- Conduct an **SEL**-related resource and needs assessment to inform goals for school-wide **SEL**.
- Design and implement effective professional learning programs to build internal capacity for academic, social, and emotional learning.
- Adopt and implement evidence-based programs for academic, social, and emotional learning across all grade levels.
- Integrate **SEL** at all three levels of school functioning (curriculum and instruction, school-wide practices and policies, family and community partnerships).
- Establish processes to continuously improve academic, social, and emotional learning through inquiry and data collection.

In addition to following the CASEL framework, Minnesota is one of the states that conduct **SEL** assessments. As is stated on their website, "To better understand how district, school, and classroom practices support the social and emotional development of all students, it is important to assess both SEL practices and outcomes" (MDE, 2020). There are various types of **SEL** assessments including outcome and process-based assessments.

Nevada

In Nevada, they have been implementing **SEL** standards since 2017 based upon Washoe County's model (NDE, u.d.). Washoe County is a forerunner school district that has been receiving extra funds from various grants to implement quality **SEL** programs. The state of Nevada saw the success of this program and decided to expand it statewide.

In the statewide social and emotional competencies explanation, it is stated that "93% of teachers believe teaching **SEL** is fairly important" (NDE, u.d.). Similar to Michigan, the state lists the competencies that students should master under each **SEL** skill. One example is for **social-awareness** students should "show empathy" and "appreciate diversity" (NDE, u.d.).

New Jersey

The state's Department of Education site has many resources for educators including the **SEL** lesson plans from the American Federation of Teachers, Edutopia, the University of British Columbia, among others (NJDE, 2020). There are also **SEL** family resources available including tool kits and fact sheets from Edutopia and other organizations (NJDE, 2020).

There is the New Jersey Alliance for Social, Emotional, and Character Development which promotes **SEL** in the state. It is the alliance's purpose to assist educators and all other stakeholders in their efforts to foster ethical, responsible, and caring people while they model and teach the social-emotional skills, ethical, and performance values that lead to good character (NJASECD, 2020).

This alliance is a network committed to educating its members regarding relevant research, implementing best practices, facilitating the exchange of resources and ideas, and advocating for the importance of a collaborative and caring organizational climate with a healthy school culture (NJASECD, 2020).

New York State

The New York State Education Department has initiated the Social and Emotional Development and Learning Guidelines (SEDL), which serves as a useful model that other states could adapt to fit their resources, priorities, and needs. These guidelines were incorporated into the Board of Regents' P-16 Plan Action 11 in 2008 as a way to reduce barriers to learning; SEDL are voluntary guidelines.

Resources are provided to school districts with information, examples, and evidence of **SEL** in elementary and secondary school education programs. SEDL argues for the necessary framework to improve the school culture within the school environment, which includes the classrooms, hallways, auditorium, cafeteria, locker rooms, playground, and the school bus. The measurement of the school culture is conducted through school climate surveys administered to educators and parents (NYSDE, 2011).

The regents have approved a local diploma option that allows the development of equivalent academic tasks, often part of a portfolio-based system that can be substituted for the Regents Examination. All local options must be reviewed and approved by the State Education Agency (SEA).

The New York Performance Standards Consortium is a group of twenty-seven secondary schools who have received a state-approved waiver allowing their students to complete a graduation portfolio in lieu of the Regents Examination in all subjects but English.

This portfolio includes a set of ambitious performance tasks—a scientific investigation, a mathematical model, a literary essay, a history/social science research paper, an arts demonstration, and a reflection on a community service or internship experience which meet a set of common standards and are scored through social moderation processes including common scoring rubrics (Performance Standards Consortium, 2013; Darling-Hammond & Adamson, 2014).

North Dakota

North Dakota has created a three-tiered learning network for schools at all stages in all processes of **SEL** implementation (NDREA, 2020). Schools self-select one of three tiers. The three tiers include an intensive group of schools that receive targeted assistance, intermediate schools that are supported in creating an implementation plan, and universal schools that are invited to semiannual **SEL** summits. Representatives from all tiers along the learning network assist state leaders in establishing resources for North Dakota schools (NDREA, 2020).

Similar to other states including **SEL** into their standards, they have created guidelines and benchmarks for each grade level. For grades 9–12, in the relationship skills category, for instance, students are expected to "evaluate personal response to conflict and create a plan for personal growth in resolving conflict" (NDREA, 2020). In responsible decision-making, they are expected to "demonstrate the ability to accurately anticipate problems in a variety of situations" (NDREA, 2020).

Rhode Island

SEL "is a process for helping children and adults develop the fundamental skills for success in life" (RIDE, 2020). Rhode Island names the competencies for school and life success. The **SEL** skill is called an anchor standard and the learning standard is listed as the expectations to achieve the skill. One example for **social awareness** is that the students should be able to "read social cues and respond appropriately" (RIDE, 2020).

These **SEL** Standards are intended to assist school staff, families, and students in identifying Social and Emotional Skills that will help students succeed. These standards were developed due to requests from school administrators, teachers, and support professionals (RIDE, 2020).

Rhode Island stresses the negative impacts of trauma and emotional stress, which will have an impact on how well a student, or adult, shows **SEL** proficiency (RIDE, 2020). When a person is under stress, anxiety, and/or is pre-occupied with an issue they perceive as a priority, they may not be able to show the same level of **social awareness** or relationship skills that they are able to otherwise.

The state provides extra supports for students with disabilities who may need more explicit or specialized instruction in **SEL** skills (RIDE, 2020). Some students may need to have skills broken down into smaller steps or may need to be given concrete examples. Some disabilities can impact how an individual communicates, processes information, makes sense of the world, picks up nonverbal cues, perceives the intention of others, and/or flexibly adjusts thoughts and behavior (RIDE, 2020).

Tennessee

Tennessee uses the **SEL** standards in their guidelines per CASEL. The guidelines include self-reflection and self-assessment suggestions for teachers to ask students to actively think about their own work. Activities and materials are encouraged to specifically provide time for reflection, self-direction, and self-monitoring. Students generate questions that lead to further inquiry and self-directed learning.

Teachers monitor their thinking to ensure that they understand the information given. Instructional plans include the following: activities, materials, and assessments that provide appropriate time for student work, student reflection, and lesson unit and closure. Assignments require students to organize, interpret, analyze, synthesize, and evaluate information rather than reproduce it (TDOE, 2015).

Washington

The American Institutes for Research (AIR) was contracted by the Washington Office of Superintendent of Public Instruction (OSPI) to create a detailed scan of a Canadian province that has developed **SEL** standards (Social Emotional Learning Indicators Workgroup, 2017). This scan informed the current Washington State's **SEL** standards, benchmarks, and indicators (SBIs).

The SBIs should be used by educators to inform instruction and student development. The SBIs can further inform administrators in supporting the needs of their teachers. Families can use them to better understand their children's **SEL** progress. Students are encouraged to use their own voice at the greatest extent possible.

SBIs are developed in conjunction with the Washington **SEL** implementation guide, which is based on the four principles that ground this work: equity, universal design, cultural responsiveness, and trauma-informed approaches (Social Emotional Learning Indicators Workgroup, 2017).

West Virginia

Within the West Virginia state standards, there is a student dispositions chapter titled "school and community social skills standards," which states that schools should support and promote **SEL** in all settings. The state department of education does not require that **SEL** be documented in individual teacher lesson plans but suggests that it should serve as a framework for school-wide student behavior expectations, which are determined by the school faculty (WVDOE, 2016).

Wisconsin

The **SEL** competencies are embedded within their Mental Health Framework. **SEL** is connected to relationship building and resiliency, trauma sensitive practices, and mental health and wellness (DPI, 2018). **SEL** is related to their goal in helping every child graduate and become college and career ready. The state focuses on keeping students healthy, safe, supported, and encouraged in schools. They promote engaged learning, inspiring and empower educators to teach while fixing the broken school funding system (DPI, 2018).

They do this by growing mental health supports for students across the state, support and expand community learning centers as safe environments for extended learning, ensure every child has access to summer learning opportunities, and enhance school safety measures that address bullying, racism, and harassment (DPI, 2018).

One study that Wisconsin references to support the inclusion of **SEL** in their standards was conducted by Columbia University which found that $11 is returned on every $1 spent on **SEL** programming. Students receiving comprehensive **SEL** instruction increase their achievement test scores by 11 percent points (CASEL, 2017).

OTHER STATES USING SEL TOOLS

Alabama

There are free standing standards for character development, but these are not comprehensive and are not developed across grade levels (CASEL, u.d.). Alabama stresses the following characteristics specifically: courage, patriotism, citizenship, honesty, fairness, respect for others, kindness, cooperation, self-respect, and perseverance (ALEX, u.d.).

The characteristics kindness, cooperation, self-respect, and perseverance are founded in the social competence and personal competence dimensions within **emotional intelligence theory**. The state mandates that ten minutes per day of character education are required for all K-12 students per the 1975 code of Alabama; the 1995 Accountability Law mandates character education. The State Board of Education and all local boards develop and implement a comprehensive character education program for all grades.

Massachusetts

Massachusetts matches their **SEL** definitions with the CASEL. The following definitions fall under this definition: **self-management**, self-awareness, **social-awareness**, responsible decision-making, and social skills, which are all justified by emotional intelligence.

School administrations conduct a needs assessment to determine what will meet the identified needs including, but not limited to, plans for professional development, the types of programs and instruction to implement at what time and how, and how progress will be assessed. Schools avoid the adoption of a random assortment of programs to address social and emotional issues.

Each school develops its own plan for **SEL** implementation and climate improvement following district-wide guidelines. The plans align across the grade levels K-12. With a coordinated approach, key elements of **SEL** serve as an organizing framework for all of a school's academic, prevention, health, and youth development activities (MADESE, u.d.).

Massachusetts uses rubrics and methods to measure the progress and impact of **SEL** programs. Massachusetts' educators use these data to inform decisions about continuing, modifying, and/or changing the future course of action. Their assessment tools measure a broad range of academic outcomes, such as higher-order thinking, analytical, creative, and practical skills.

Their instruments are necessary not only for the measurement of **SEL** implementation but also for outcomes. These tools allow a school to identify which **SEL** competencies are already present in other curricula, such as health and prevention education. Self-assessment tools for administrators, teachers, and other users provide information on the degree and fidelity of implementation.

The tools assist schools in understanding the extent to which schools and classroom environments are supportive of **SEL**. The Massachusetts Department of Elementary and Secondary Education (MADESE) suggests that all schools help their students meet their established **SEL** standards and engage in regular assessment of their progress. For instance, the MADESE guidebook for inclusive practice aligns **SEL** with educator rubrics to include guiding frameworks.

Respondents to interviews conducted by a Rennie Center Report (2015) about **SEL** implementation in Massachusetts noted that the addition of **SEL** assessments was discouraged due to a high number of assessments in general. As there are still **SEL** assessments emerging, the Rennie report suggested that each district and school pursue **SEL** in its own way.

When implementing **SEL**, it is best for the districts to have the freedom to select their own programs to address their local needs such as behavioral problems. Nonetheless, the report stated that in Fall River, students take surveys that include various **SEL** indicators. The district also surveyed other stakeholders such as parents and teachers about topics like school climate and student performance. Although data is self-reported, and, therefore, cannot independently measure growth, respondents cited them as a key window into **SEL** progress.

Missouri

Missouri's Performance Goals within their Show-Me Standards stress more than just the main content subject areas; their emphasis is on college and career ready traits to prepare students for further education, work, and civic responsibilities (MODESE, u.d.).

There are four goals that link knowledge and performance to the goal of academic success. The first goal is for students to acquire the knowledge and skills to gather, analyze, and apply information and ideas. The second goal is for students to acquire the knowledge and skills to communicate effectively within and beyond the classroom. The third goal is for students to acquire the knowledge and skills to recognize and solve problems. The fourth goal is for students to acquire the knowledge and skills to make decisions and act as responsible members of society.

These standards are not a curriculum; rather, they serve as guidelines for local school districts to reference when addressing challenging curriculum to help all students achieve their maximum potential. Missouri law assures local control of education; each school district will determine how its curriculum will be structured with the best methods to implement it in the classroom (MODESE, u.d.).

Pennsylvania

The Pennsylvania Department of Education (PDOE, 2016) promotes School-Family Partnership Strategies to enhance children's social, emotional, and academic growth in grades K-12. The partnership places attention on self-awareness, building and maintaining positive relationships, belief in oneself, cooperation, communication, responsible decision-making, and **self-management** which are all affiliated with Goleman's emotional intelligence.

School-Family Partnerships (SFP) is a collaboration with student's adult caretakers to create an engaging and supportive climate for learning both in school and at home. Administrators and educators apply an SFP framework to **SEL** programming through the use of educator distributed surveys, interviews or home visits, icebreakers, and other related activities to learn more about students and their families. Teachers might ask students and families about likes and dislikes, special talents and skills, family composition, and concerns or areas for improvement.

In addition to the SFP and **SEL** focus in Pennsylvania, the state has academic standards for career education and work. These standards emphasize the following core areas: career awareness and preparation; career acquisition; career retention and advancement; and entrepreneurship. The most relevant to CCR is career retention and advancement where the following areas are a concern: work habits, cooperation, and teamwork; group interaction; budgeting; time management; workplace changes; and lifelong learning.

Pennsylvania uses implementation assessments, which are surveys that identify what teachers do to address career education and work standards and how students are responding to its inclusion into their curriculum. For instance, the student questionnaires ask about their collaboration skills used to accomplish projects. The assessment survey asks teachers whether or not their students are using conflict resolution skills as they relate to the workplace such as constructive criticism, group dynamics, leadership, mediation, negotiation, and problem-solving.

Pennsylvania has a career education and work standards NOCTI assessment that was created just for the state. The assessment was developed based on a statewide competency task list and contained multiple-choice and performance-based components; the assessment measures technical skills at the occupational level.

PURPOSE OF STATE STANDARDS

All the aforementioned states provide at least some standards that align with the **SEL** competencies; it is up to the discretion of the state which competencies they wish to develop within their students. The differences lay within the varying types of characteristics they deem necessary for college and career success.

The states with the most commonalities include the following: Illinois, Massachusetts, Pennsylvania, Tennessee, and West Virginia due to their focus on the traditional **SEL** competencies, which correspond the most with the **emotional intelligence theory**. The majority of the states focus on the personal competence dimension of the **emotional intelligence theory** and is linked with **growth mindset** and internal motivation. Alabama is the only state that includes character education, which differs from the traditional **SEL** competencies.

Most states do not have evidence of implementation and outcomes; therefore, the extent to which states, districts, and individuals schools implement **SEL** is uncertain (Fried et al., 2015). In some states, there are clear **SEL** standards and developmental benchmarks; however, implementation is at the discretion of the school districts' leadership (Fried et al., 2015). The integration of **SEL** into accountability systems will drive change in practice, but a lack of political will may also hinder the effort.

The **SEL** standards are currently guiding many states' **SEL** programs. There have been many changes to the **SEL** standards in the last several years, particularly from 2017 to 2018. For instance, in that time frame, ten more states have decided to include **SEL** standards because they are quickly seeing their value. Most states that have incorporated **SEL** standards have **SEL** guidelines and benchmarks for age or grade levels based upon CASEL's **SEL** definition. **SEL** assessments aid in determining both the effectiveness of the **SEL** programs and standards.

QUESTIONS FOR TEACHERS

1. How can teachers use the **SEL** standards to inform instruction?
2. How can the **SEL** benchmarks and guidelines help educators rather than overwhelm them?
3. How can performance-based assessments be used to evaluate **SEL** competencies in students?

QUESTIONS FOR SCHOOL LEADERS

1. How can the **SEL** standards of my state or another state inform school initiatives?
2. If my state does not have **SEL** standards, how may I suggest their inclusion at my school district?
3. How can **SEL** assessments inform the effectiveness of **SEL** standards, including guidelines and benchmarks?

ADDITIONAL RESOURCE

Scan Scorecard Project

CASEL provided a scan of each state's **SEL** standards including guidelines and benchmarks. CASEL has been monitoring each state's inclusion since 2015. There have been many changes to state standards since 2017 (CASEL, 2016, u.d.)

ALEX. (u.d.). Retrieved from http://alex.state.al.us/standardAll.php?subject=CE&summary=1.
CASEL. (2016). State scan scorecard project. Retrieved from http://www.casel.org/state-scan-scorecard-project.
CASEL. (2017). What is SEL. Retrieved from http://www.casel.org/what-is-sel/.
CASEL. (u.d.). Scan scorecard project. Retrieved from http://www.casel.org/state-scan-scorecard-project.
CDC. (2016). Healthy schools. Retrieved from http://www.cdc.gov/healthyschools/sher/standards/4.htm.
CEP. (2013). *How is career readiness assessed?* Retrieved from Washington, DC: http://www.cep-dc.org/data/searchquery.cfm?search=Yes.
Common Core State Standards. (2016). English language arts standards. Retrieved from http://www.corestandards.org/ELA-Literacy/introduction/key-design-consideration/.
Darling-Hammond, & Adamson. (2014). *Beyond the bubble test: How performance assessments support 21st century learning.* San Francisco, CA: Jossey-Bass.
(2018). SEL webinar. Retrieved from https://www.youtube.com/channel/UC-LOv-L2VbEzKpxXkSZsIAA.
Fried, Poulos, Culbertson, Chalmers, & D'Entremont. (2015). *Social and emotional learning: Opportunities for Massachusetts, lessons for the nation.* Boston, MA: Rennie Center Education Research and Policy.
Friedman, Kern, Hampson, & Duckworth. (2014). A new lifespan approach to conscientiousness and health: Combining the pieces of the causal puzzle. *Development and Psychology, 50*(5), 1377–1389.
Garcia, & Emma. (2014). *The need to address noncognitive skills in the education policy agenda. Briefing Paper #386.* Retrieved from http://proxygw.wrlc.org/login?url=http://search.ebscohost.com/login.aspx?direct=true&db=eric&AN=ED558126&site=ehost-live.
ISBE. (2013). Illinois early learning and development standards preschool. Retrieved from http://www.isbe.state.il.us/earlychi/pdf/early_learning_standards.pdf.

ISBE. (2016). Illinois learning standards social/emotional learning (SEL). Retrieved from http://www.isbe.net/ils/social_emotional/standards.htm.

KDOE. (u.d.). School counseling – Social, emotional and character development. Retrieved from http://www.ksde.org/Agency/Division-of-Learning-Services/Career-Standards-and-Assessment-Services/Content-Area-M-Z/School-Counseling/Social-Emotional-and-Character-Development.

MADESE. (u.d.). Guidelines on the implementation of social and emotional learning (SEL) curricula K-12. Retrieved from http://www.doe.mass.edu/bullying/SELguide.pdf.

MDE. (2017). Michigan Department of Education early childhood to grade 12 social and emotional learning (SEL) competencies and indicators. Retrieved from https://drive.google.com/file/d/1qovbNTK_DQGbg3eXQV0ZRdPlLK33ueth/view.

MDE. (2020). SEL implementation guidance. Retrieved from https://education.mn.gov/MDE/dse/safe/social/imp/.

MDOE. (u.d.). Guiding principles. Retrieved from http://www.maine.gov/doe/proficiency/standards/guiding-principles.html.

MODESE. (u.d.). Show-me standards. Retrieved from https://dese.mo.gov/show-me-standards.

NDE. (u.d.). Nevada statewide social and emotional competencies. Retrieved from https://drive.google.com/file/d/1ccfXOeLiNcCUvjD8gdI8u32EwxBgqUWR/view.

NDREA. (2020). Statewide initiatives. Retrieved from http://www.ndrea.org/index.php?id=103.

NJASECD. (2020). New Jersey Alliance for social, emotional, and character development. Retrieved from http://www.njasecd.org/.

NJDE. (2020). Keeping our kids safe, healthy & in school. Retrieved from https://www.state.nj.us/education/students/safety/sandp/sel/.

NYSDE. (2011). Guidelines and resources for social and emotional development and learning: Educating the whole child engaging the whole world. Retrieved from http://www.regents.nysed.gov/common/regents/files/documents/meetings/2011Meetings/June2011/11p12d1.pdf.

PDOE. (2016). Pennsylvania Department of Education standards aligned system. Retrieved from https://www.pdesas.org.

Performance Standards Consortium. (2013). *Educating for the 21st century: Data report on the New York Performance Standards Consortium*. Retrieved from New York, NY: http://performanceassessment.org/articles/DataReport_NY_PSC.pdf.

RIDE. (2020). Social & emotional learning (SEL). Retrieved from https://www.ride.ri.gov/StudentsFamilies/HealthSafety/SocialEmotionalLearning.aspx.

Social Emotional Learning Indicators Workgroup. (2017). Social emotional learning standards benchmarks and indicators. Retrieved from https://www.k12.wa.us/sites/default/files/public/studentsupport/sel/pubdocs/Appendix%20D%20Standards%2C%20Benchmarks%20Indicators.pdf.

TDOE. (2015). Incorporating social and emotional learning into classroom instruction and educator effectiveness: A toolkit for Tennessee teachers and administrators. Retrieved from https://www.tn.gov/assets/entities/education/attachments/safe_sch_se_toolkit.pdf.

WVDOE. (2016). Policy 4373 electronic manual. Retrieved from http://wvde.state.wv.us/healthyschools/ElectronicManual4373New.html#Selfaw%20enessandSelfmanagement.

Chapter 4

Arguments against SEL Assessments in School Accountability

The ability to recognize student **SEL** growth can be useful for states and districts moving forward with their policies regarding **SEL** inclusion in **school accountability** systems. **SEL** needs to be monitored in curriculum and practice. Schools need supports for effective **SEL** inclusion. Key takeaways can be learned from educators and administrators who interact with **SEL** on a daily basis. Now is the time to address **SEL** as it becomes more popular; nonetheless, it is essential to understand both sides of the argument toward inclusion of **SEL** and against.

CONCERNS ABOUT THE INCLUSION OF SEL IN SCHOOL ACCOUNTABILITY

Federal and state laws driven by NCLB (2002) promoted cognitive skills and standardized testing over **SEL** skills, making it essential to map out the counterargument for using **SEL**. Self-reports and teacher reports are a common measure for **SEL** and a possible method of inclusion in **school accountability** systems. Some researchers argue that **SEL** should not be included in **school accountability** systems.

Duckworth, known for her research on the importance of "grit" as an attribute of perseverance, and Yeager, a researcher with extensive contributions in the field of "growth mindsets," detailed concerns about the inclusion of **SEL** skills in **school accountability** systems. They argue that potential flaws exist in every measurement tool used to track the effectiveness of **SEL** traits, and such evaluations should not be used for accountability measures like school-to-school comparisons or teacher evaluations, which bring negative consequences (Duckworth & Yeager, 2015).

Flaws of concern include the following: (1) Survey participants may interpret questions differently from how researchers intended; (2) students or teachers may be limited in their ability to answer questions about growth in internal traits such as motivation; (3) surveys may fail to detect smaller incremental changes; (4) **reference bias** may lead to different results from similar respondents; (5) "social desirability bias" may lead students to give answers they think teachers want to see in response to certain questions rather than answering honestly; and (6) teachers may make assumptions about students when evaluating their behavior.

For example, if they have determined that a student is a "good kid," they may assume high levels of self-control, without proof (Blad, 2015; Duckworth & Yeager, 2015). Considerations such as performance tasks may explain student choices and rationale. Children in the delay-of-gratification task wait longer if they trust that the experimenter will actually later deliver on the promise of two marshmallows (Kidd et al., 2013). Likewise, performance on self-control tasks can be affected when performed after difficult tasks (Hagger et al., 2010).

The precision of self-control assessments is in question because of these circumstances, which influence individual students differently. For example, a difficult task may be perceived as a positive learning experience by one student and as a challenge to avoid by another.

Teacher reports of personal characteristics may be accurate within the respective schools, such as when comparing classes in the same school. This more readily assures that the standard for a given characteristic is held constant. However, when between-school program evaluations are conducted—as is fairly popular—self-report and teacher-report questionnaires could be biased (Duckworth & Yeager, 2015). For instance, teachers at schools with more rigorous behavior standards may assess their students more harshly.

Researchers, such as West, agreed with Duckworth and Yeager about the limitations of including **SEL** in **school accountability** systems. One limitation of **SEL** questionnaires: students are subject to faking, and therefore, to **social desirability bias** West (2014).

When considering whether an item such as "I am a hard worker" should be marked "very much like me," a child (or his or her teacher or parent) may be inclined to choose a higher rating in order to appear more attractive to others or assume the best in their child. This tendency will inflate individual responses but not alter their rank order. If some individuals respond more to social pressure than others, however, their placement within the overall distribution of responses could change.

Reference bias, which occurs when survey responses are influenced by differing standards of comparison, is troublesome West (2014). A child deciding whether she is a hard worker must conjure up a mental image of hard work with which she can compare her own habits.

A child with high standards might consider a hard worker to be someone who does his or her homework well before bedtime and, in addition, organizes and reviews his or her notes from the day's classes. Another child might consider a hard worker to be someone who brings home his or her assignments and attempts to complete them, even if most of them remain unfinished the next morning (West, 2014). The effects of evaluations for the educator, school, and family influence on **SEL** skills could lead to false conclusions if the assessments are interpreted through distinct frames of reference (West, 2014).

Better measures than student self-reports are less susceptible to **reference bias**. They suggested measuring students' nonacademic skills but recommended doing so in full recognition of the flaws of the current measures. In addition to West, Yeager, and Duckworth, there are many researchers who argue that **SEL** should not be included in **school accountability** systems.

Given the limits of various types of **SEL** assessments, experts suggest using a multimethod approach to measurement. This approach may dramatically increase reliability and validity of **SEL** (Eid & Diener, 2006; Rushton et al., 1983). For example, aggregated multiple measures of self-control, including a delay-of-gratification task and self-report, teacher-report, and parent-report questionnaires Duckworth and Seligman (2005). They discovered that a composite score for self-control in the fall predicted final report card grades better than a standard measure of cognitive ability. They also encouraged further innovation in measurement development.

An incomplete list of promising approaches includes mining students' online learning behavior or written communication in real time (e.g., Twitter feeds, Kahn Academy databases) for meaningful patterns of behavior (Friedman et al., 2014; Ireland & Pennebaker, 2010).

Based upon the **SEL** assessments, preliminary analyses from the CORE pilot program indicate that there is strong reliability of **SEL** inclusion in curriculum and **school accountability**. Furthermore, **SEL** inclusion within curriculum is positively associated with higher academic performance and behavior, both across and within schools. Nonetheless, these preliminary findings do not indicate how students would perform in all settings.

Unfortunately, there is no example of how **SEL** assessments have been administered in a high-stake setting because of the modest weight that is attached to each **SEL** assessment within the pilot program. The stakes that are attached to these assessments may determine future funding, continuation, and a redoing of **school accountability**.

The current weight of **SEL** assessments in **school accountability** impacts the way that teachers and administrators think about the results of these assessments had they not been included in **school accountability**. There is not substantial weight given to these assessments to make strong judgments about their overall impact on **school accountability**.

Additionally, there is little to no evidence on the reliability of **SEL** measures. Duckworth and Yeager aggregated to the school level so that they could distinguish between schools with high and low levels of performance. **Reference bias** might lead to inferences that are misleading about certain schools with particularly distinctive environments.

EVIDENCE SUPPORTING INCLUSION OF SEL ASSESSMENTS IN SCHOOL ACCOUNTABILITY

As a policy initiative, **SEL** is not without controversy. There are positive and negative arguments about including **SEL** in **school accountability** systems. Engagement correlated with positive academic outcomes (Fredricks et al., 2004). Noted outcomes include student achievement and persistence at the school level, which was higher in classrooms with supportive teachers and peers who engage and motivate students.

There is growing evidence that school programs focused explicitly on **SEL** also support student achievement. Analyses by researchers at CASEL (2003) found that students who received **SEL** programming embedded within school curriculum academically outperformed their peers who did not have access to **SEL** programming.

These data were gathered from eighty-seven **SEL** programs across the country that met CASEL's four main criteria: the program is school based and has sequenced lessons for a general student population; there are at least eight lessons in one of the program years; there are at least two consecutive grade spans; and the program is nationally available and provided CASEL the materials for review (CASEL, 2003).

When students had access to **SEL** programming, they earned improved grades and graduated at higher rates. Moreover, effective **SEL** programming instilled social outcomes such as positive peer relationships, caring and empathy, and social engagement. **SEL** instruction also led to reductions in problem behavior within schools such as drug use, violence, and delinquency (CASEL, 2003).

The evidence suggests that **SEL**, as implemented through these programs, may produce positive outcomes for students. It suggests that, given these correlations, the inclusion of **SEL** within **school accountability** systems may ensure that educators improve their academic achievement. Approximately 50 percent of skills needed for **high school** and college academic success are social-emotional (Steinberg, 2014). Some even argue that a higher percentage of skills fall into the social-emotional category (Rothstein, 2014).

In assessing academic knowledge, it is not simply a question of whether performances on **SEL** assessments as effective as standardized academic exams. Rather, it is whether such assessments are necessary to assess students' communication skills, confidence, discipline, and the ability to adapt to unforeseen situations (Rothstein, 2014).

Both types of assessments are needed for a holistic approach to accountability. Scholars claim that **SEL** skills are as important, if not more so, than academic knowledge (Steinberg, 2014). For instance, in a study undertaken in direct response to NCLB, teacher and parent ratings of children's self-control in fourth grade were far better predictors of ninth grade GPA than fourth grade IQ tests (Duckworth et al., 2012).

Furthermore, a better indicator of college graduation rates than standardized testing is grade point average because it demonstrates the ability for students to be challenged and succeed over a period of time (Tanner, 2014).

In sum, **SEL** has the longevity and ability to improve student academic achievement.

One factor that influences how adolescent students learn new skills is developmental, specifically their malleability during adolescence (ages 12–18). Neuroscience has shown that adolescence is a second period of heightened brain plasticity or development (Bandura, 2001). Brain regions considered important for the development of essential **SEL** skills also were among the most malleable (Bandura, 2001).

The rationale behind teaching **SEL** to adolescents, in particular, is that they can improve these particular skills during this crucial formative period. To foster success in **high school** students, schools need to develop the **SEL** traits that will help motivate them to complete their college degrees. Currently, students are not positively challenged enough (Tough, 2012). They need to develop a sense of how they think and behave so that they may attain traits such as self-determination, self-control, and perseverance, which allow them to complete their college degrees and achieve their career of interest (Steinberg, 2014).

The issue is not the number of students enrolling in college, but the number of students persisting to graduation. **SEL** skills—namely, self-awareness, **self-management, social-awareness**, and social skills—are likely to bridge the barriers to achieve success.

SEL ATTRIBUTES IN COLLEGE AND WORKPLACE SUCCESS

College admissions, job placement, and self-assessment exams increasingly incorporate **SEL** assessments. Workplaces have used **SEL** testing to save on the cost of hiring and training future employees. Workforce training is a $50-billion industry in the United States alone (Kyllonen, 2012). Employers also value college education because of the preparation it provides students for the workplace. **SEL** skills development can predict workplace outcomes in addition to predicting academic success.

For instance, researchers found a correlation between the **SEL** skills in eighth grade boys and their employment twenty years later. In a National Educational Longitudinal Study (NELS) in 2012, which used data from 1988 and 1990, a national probability sample of teachers was asked to rate students on the following:

- Timeliness of completing homework
- Attendance
- Tardiness
- Attentiveness
- Behavior, including disruption

Survey results found that 55 percent of the students had misbehaved and that misbehavior ratings predicted lower educational attainment and lower earnings at ages twenty-six and twenty-seven (Kyllonen, 2012). In addition, eighth grade achievement test scores predicted earnings at ages twenty-six and twenty-seven, but only for degree holders (Kyllonen, 2012).

In 2000 and 2001, studies were conducted about the University of Michigan's alternate assessment system for business school admissions. The purpose of the assessment system was to test two new measures—a situational judgment test and a case-based problem test to be administered to business school applicants along with the GMAT (Kyllonen, 2012).

The test measured cognitive ability by asking longer problems that required reflection and judgment, or "practical intelligence." Although the findings did not correlate as highly as the GMAT for business school grades, they were able to forecast other outcomes, such as project grades and attainment of leadership positions, that the GMAT did not predict.

This information is pertinent because of **SEL**'s link to other outcomes, such as leadership roles, which a standardized test could not predict. **SEL** assessments help educators monitor all students, especially those who have the hidden potential to succeed. These assessments give educators the insight to equip all students with the resources to make their successes a reality.

Some relevant studies conducted outside of education draw on economics. These studies focus on specific labor markets and workplace preparation, which demonstrate the importance of teaching **SEL** skills in school for success in the workforce. For instance, research links the effects of socio-emotional personality and personal background to unemployment rates or hiring practices.

Specifically, unemployment policies targeting individuals with poor family backgrounds should help reduce the role of differing soft skills, such as perseverance, mindset, and social skills, and their influence during childhood and early adulthood (Lee et al., 2015). These employment-oriented studies demonstrate the need for CCR building skills within schools to mitigate issues later in life. It is for these reasons that education policymakers advance the option to states and districts to include measurements of **SEL** skills and dispositions within **school accountability** systems.

The uneven development of **SEL** skills among students contributes to the achievement gap that separates wealthy students from their disadvantaged peers (West et al., 2014). This signifies that disadvantaged students are less likely to have the **SEL** skills needed to perform well in school. Social-emotional ability among students affects their acquisition of the skills needed for workplace productivity, including positive behavior skills considered more important than traditional academic abilities in terms of performance, both academic and professional (Heckman et al., 2006).

THE PERSPECTIVES OF SCHOOL PRINCIPALS AND EDUCATORS IN SCHOOL ACCOUNTABILITY

To truly understand the integration of **SEL** into curriculum, assessments, and **school accountability** systems, educator perspectives provide hidden and potentially useful information that statistics cannot provide. Relationships among educators, administrators, and students must be nurtured to establish a positive culture that is pervasive in the learning community. It is through these relationships that true school transformation can occur. This positive culture provides a foundation for the exchange of beliefs, values, knowledge, and skills.

SEL provides a basis for quality learning and outcomes, which are essential for integrative learning and overall human development (Bird & Sultmann, 2010). **SEL** helps build personal and group completeness, which strengthens relationships central to all interaction and learning.

It is insightful to understand educator perspectives on **school accountability** to find out which accountability criteria are effective and feasible. Teachers were surveyed to understand their perceptions of the state accountability system in South Carolina (Berryhill et al., 2009). The teachers cited burnout as their most significant reaction to the high demands of standardized test scores in their accountability systems.

Educators also feel that policymakers do not understand their role because they do not have enough interactions with teachers and classrooms

(Berryhill et al., 2009). Participating teachers suggested policymakers should interact more with teachers to make better policy decisions. Teachers suggested reducing the demands of their job and increasing resources, reducing class size, adding teacher aides, and updating materials and equipment (Berryhill et al., 2009).

Positive relationships with educators and peers yield a quality education for all students. It is not always obvious to educators how these relationships can be nurtured amid an overpacked curriculum, increasing accountability, and more expectations.

SEL reinforces the cultural link between the vision and mission of a school and its adoption within the wider school community (Clark & Clark, 2006). **School accountability** is complex for school leaders who must be personally and professionally accountable from both an ethical and political perspective, beyond just the numbers (Clark & Clark, 2006).

Educators sense the increasing pressures for accountability, which may reduce school curricular options and restrict school autonomy. Educators can use the data from testing to determine which students require the most help and in which subject matter; however, this is also true of **SEL** assessments. In the time of quality school reform, it is necessary to engage in interactive information exchange that values teacher input (Lewis, 2004).

When teachers processed information about school reform, they attached little emotion to the facts; however, when they processed the very same information about their own classroom, teachers experienced a more emotional connection (Schmidt & Datnow, 2005). Therefore, it is essential to consider how high-stake assessments and a stressful work environment influence teachers' beliefs and attitudes (Ransford, 2007).

Some educators report that accountability via high-stakes testing limits student success to a single measure. Researchers also find that one state test does not properly measure learning, which is likely a result of limited understanding (Clark & Clark, 2006).

In regards to principal leadership behaviors, there is a positive relationship in elementary teachers' perceptions of their principals' inviting leadership behaviors, such as frequent communication and school climate surveys (Egley, 2005). Consequently, the manner in which principals interact with their faculty correlates with the achievement level of their students. While many factors affect student achievement, inviting leadership behaviors are an important component of quality schools that receive **high school accountability** rankings (Egley, 2005).

Researchers experience difficulty in determining specific school-level characteristics that have an impact on student achievement. For instance, a study of a diverse sample of twenty-four middle schools examined differences among schools rated as exemplary, recognized, academically acceptable, and academically unacceptable (Jackson & Lunenburg, 2010).

These school rankings were assessed using four performance indicator dimensions: academic excellence, developmental responsiveness, social equity, and organizational structures. **School accountability** ratings, student achievement scores, and demographic characteristics were obtained from the state department of education. All four performance indicator dimensions experienced significant differences (Jackson & Lunenburg, 2010).

Ethical accountability requires a school culture of values and beliefs among students to create trusting relationships, learning, assessment, collaborative decision-making, and shared leadership. Strong, trusting relationships between teachers and students and between teachers and principals are essential for producing positive learning environments (Clark & Clark, 2006).

Principals should build caring relationships with staff and understand professional needs in order to treat their staff equitably. Additionally, the celebration of individual and group successes are among the leaders' responsibilities that lead to higher student achievement (Goldwyn, 2007).

Principal leadership responsibilities involve human interactions, culture, visibility, contingent rewards, input, affirmation, and relationships (Clark & Clark, 2006). Even with the pressure of high-stakes testing within **school accountability**, educators cite that principals have high levels of inviting leadership behaviors (Egley, 2005). Many principals emphasize just improving test scores; meanwhile, research underscores the importance of maintaining an inviting climate for educators and students that promotes respect, trust, and optimism (Egley, 2005).

Qualitative researchers conduct comparative case studies of schools of high- and low-performing schools (Jackson & Lunenburg, 2010). This suggestion was made because of the need to analyze the following: how these schools look in practice; the differences that exist among them; and the experiences of students, teachers, and parents. These prospective studies would determine how effective the culture is for learning. These aforementioned performance indicator dimensions furthermore provide the potential for students to overcome the influence of socioeconomic status (Jackson & Lunenburg, 2010).

Political accountability and the assessment of standards are based on limited evidence of student learning, as they draw from a student's performance on standardized tests. Educators recognize the importance of their students doing well on these exams and are concerned that so much relies on a unilateral measure of student learning.

Parents, community members, and business and political leaders share the belief that academic outcomes on standardized tests indicate student learning and success. Politically knowledgeable principals, however, understand that the community at large values and seeks these measures. Their efforts to ensure that their students meet the requirements improve their credibility within their communities (Clark & Clark, 2006).

Leaders of successful schools accept accountability, and they do not make the mistake of restricting it to state and district mandates. They understand that these mandates must be met, yet they also realize that their job demands accountability beyond standardized testing (Clark & Clark, 2004; Uskali, 2004; Valentine et al., 2004). Often the purposes of accountability benchmarks are for the promotion of student learning, the improvement of parent and community relationships, and the implementation of the curriculum standards in specific subject areas.

Politically savvy principals build political capital by taking an active role in understanding how to develop responsive programs and organize structures with multiple assessment procedures (Clark & Clark, 2006). State accountability programs have the greatest impact on monitoring student academic achievement (Lyons & Algozzine, 2006). **School accountability** achieves this impact through aligning curriculum to the testing program, providing student remedial or tutorial opportunities, assigning highly qualified teachers to grade levels or subjects, and protecting instructional time (Lyons & Algozzine, 2006).

Principals with political acumen take an active role in understanding the development of responsive programs, school organizational structure, and multiple assessment procedures to build capacity among their staff and community. **SEL** is just one resource principals can use to shape school culture.

From understanding these programs, broad-based support and accountability systems can develop while also enhancing learning opportunities

(Valentine et al., 2004). Instructional strategies that help teachers increase student learning include identifying similarities and differences among students, students receiving reinforcement for effort and recognition for this achievement, summarizing and note taking, completing homework and practicing, using linguistic representations, and learning cooperatively (Goldwyn, 2007; Jackson & Lunenburg, 2010).

Even though principals recognize previous changes in legislation such as NCLB as unpopular, they understand the potential for increased support of programs and professional development (Bracey, 2005; Jones, 2005). Other federal and state programs support commonly held visions that their schools support successful learning for students (Valentine et al., 2004).

Ultimately, principals practice political accountability by supporting required standards and the measurement process by encouraging learning to be more comprehensive than the standards suggest. Accountability for learning involves many stakeholders, such as students, teachers, administrators, parents, community members, and policymakers. Principals further recognize that using all available resources (federal, state, local, public, and private) increases the learning opportunities for students in their schools (Clark & Clark, 2006).

Principals have networks from which they access resources to ensure that they are properly making sense of accountability and choice systems. The way in which principals interpret accountability systems affects their participation within these networks. Once activated, principal networks provide access to instrumental resources (Jennings, 2010).

Schools are also working to institutionalize sophisticated practices that foster twenty-first-century knowledge and skill acquisition by using baseline systems and practices (Szczesiul et al., 2015). Educator buy-in and support for components of accountability are essential to implementation and achieving desired results. Accountability measures also provide data, which are necessary for school leaders to make decisions.

SCHOOL REFORM SUCCESS STANDARDS

There are several criteria used by policymakers to determine effective schools. These criteria include effectiveness, popularity, and fidelity. Two less popular criteria are adaptability and longevity. A school's reform journey consists of constant adaption. For success to occur, a school needs buy-in, professional development, and resources.

In the beginning era of school reforms in the 1970s, few educators or public officials questioned new programs that received public funding as a means to cope with unmet needs for children (Cuban, 1998). Researchers and reformers assessed how well the innovations reflected their intentions. The effectiveness standard is measured by the quantifiable results of the intended reform: were the goals of the reform attained? The popularity standard is used to evaluate success because a reform receives more support if it permeates throughout the media and society as a valued change (Cuban, 1998).

The fidelity standard assesses if the reform occurred in the manner the reformers intended. It is difficult to determine the effectiveness standard when the reform departs from the initial plan. What is especially important to educators is that they can place their own design on the mandated reform and apply it to their lessons and students. The adaptability standard is the opposite of the fidelity standard in that modifications are perceived as positive indications of innovation (Cuban, 1998).

The longevity standard is the durability of a reform and can be used to determine its success or failure. Although the more common standards dominate mainstream policy formation and analysis, they are infrequently applied to social and political goals that schools are asked to achieve (Cuban, 1998). This complicates the ability to assess whether or not a school reform was truly successful in the social and political school reform changes.

OVERVIEW OF SEL'S ROLE IN SCHOOL ACCOUNTABILITY

Emotional intelligence theory supports that **SEL** be integrated into schools and be measured because it has an impact on student academic achievement. The theory supports this notion because of the personal competencies associated with **SEL**, **self-management**, and **self-efficacy**.

SEL had been called non-cognitive in many states prior to 2014, which confused many educators and was therefore the nomenclature was changed. Economists commonly refer to soft skills as **noncognitive skills**, and educators commonly refer to these same skills as whole child education or **SEL**. Traditional academic skill assessments do not measure these skills, but **SEL** skills can improve student academic achievement. Factors such as motivation, time management, and self-regulation are imperative for later life outcomes, including success in the workforce. Social investments in the development of these factors generate high return in improved educational outcomes, including diminished disparities in school performance, educational attainment, and reduced racial, ethnic, and gender disparities (Rosen et al., 2010).

The effect of these skills is comparable in magnitude to socioeconomic status and cognitive ability. **SEL** factors influence employment, occupation choice, and a variety of other labor market outcomes. Most studies assessing **SEL** used specific measurement tools, such as student reports of motivation from questionnaires. **SEL** assessments can be used in college admissions, job placement, and self-assessment. These assessments predict not only academic outcomes but workplace outcomes as well.

There is a persistent controversy about the appropriateness of including **SEL** measures in **school accountability** systems. Education research experts cannot agree. Duckworth and Yeager recently recommended that **SEL** should not be included in **school accountability** systems as it is not possible to account accurately for their validity.

Conversely, other psychology experts, such as Steinberg, encourage their inclusion due to their demonstrated positive effect on student academic outcomes (Steinberg, 2014). Until the controversy and validity of **SEL** assessments are resolved, a legislative controversy will also persist. Federal and state mandate disagreements over the inclusion of **SEL** skills in **school accountability** systems continue because of the lack of agreement from the experts.

Nonetheless, because of their popularity in both the academic and media settings, legislation within ESSA in December 2015 allows the state option to include school quality indicators and **SEL** competencies in their **school accountability** systems. States determine which to include and how to include these competencies. There are current state examples of **SEL** inclusion in state standards and examples within the literature of the roles of successful principals and educators, which can serve as a useful model for implementation into **school accountability** systems.

There is an inconsistency within school districts that initiatives nationwide aim to address. More empirical evidence of the results from **SEL** assessments is necessary to determine the efficacy of the new measurement. The various **SEL** assessments currently in use will need to be reassessed and evaluated.

Nonetheless, it is discouraging that one of the most respected researchers who also created one of these assessments, Duckworth, does not recommend their inclusion in **school accountability** systems. Although it is clear from the research that these measures have an impact on student success rates, it is less evident that these assessments are accurate enough to be included in the rankings and comparisons of schools, districts, and states.

Given recent research developments with **SEL** and the integration of **SEL** into **school accountability**, there is an increased need to know how administrators and teachers interact with **SEL**. It is illuminating to understand how they recognize growth and how they monitor and integrate **SEL** into their everyday routines, curriculum, and practice. Schools have received a long prescription of what policies they are supposed to follow but with very little description and understanding, particularly the development of social skills among staff and students.

There may be hidden policies on **SEL** that are currently being practiced that could inform others within the district and outside it. There is also much to be learned from those interacting with **SEL** who have intimate knowledge about its effectiveness and limitations. Additional research and consideration of **SEL** may be required to determine its unquestioned usability in assessing **school accountability**.

The school reform that is occurring with **SEL** is popular in the media and among most educators. It is the fidelity and effectiveness of the **SEL** assessments within the **school accountability** that will be determined in time.

QUESTIONS FOR TEACHERS

1. How could teachers remain unbiased while conducting teacher reports of student performance in **SEL**?
2. What are the best methods for creating **SEL** lessons that are aligned with the school's **SEL** program or school culture?
3. How can teachers best communicate value of **SEL** competencies for later in life outcomes to their students?

QUESTIONS FOR SCHOOL LEADERS

1. How can administrators take into account student and teacher bias in **SEL** assessments?

2. What are the best methods for providing **SEL** lessons or sample lessons to teachers that are aligned with the school's **SEL** program or school culture?
3. How can administrators improve staff culture to promote an inviting culture for educators and students?

ADDITIONAL RESOURCE

Should Noncognitive Skills be Included in School Accountability Systems?

The most concerted effort to deploy common measures of **SEL** skills as part of a **school accountability** is occurring in the California Office to Reform Education (CORE) Districts (West, 2016). These findings provide an encouraging view of the potential for self-reports of social-emotional skills as measures for evaluating school performance (West, 2016). However, they do not address how self-report measures of social-emotional skills would perform in a high-stakes environment even with the modest weight attached to them within CORE (West, 2016).

Bandura. (2001). Social cognitive theory: An agentic perspective. *Annual Review of Psychology, 52*, 1–26.

Berryhill, Linney, & Fromewick. (2009). The effects of education accountability on teachers: Are policies too-stress provoking for their own good? *International Journal of Education Policy and Leadership, 4*(5), 1–14.

Bird, & Sultmann. (2010). Social and emotional learning: Reporting a system approach to developing relationships, nurturing well-being and invigorating learning. *Educational & Child Psychology, 27*(1), 143–155.

Blad. (2015). Researchers: Measures of traits like 'grit' should not be used for accountability. *Education Week*. Retrieved from http://blogs.edweek.org/edweek/rulesforengagement/2015/05/grit_accountability_noncognitive_skills_duckworth_yeager.html?print=1.

Bracey. (2005). The 15th Bracey report on the condition of public education. *Phi Delta Kappan, 87*, 138–153.

CASEL. (2003). Safe and sound: An educational leader's guide to evidence-based social and emotional learning (SEL) programs. Retrieved from http://indiana.edu/~pbisin/pdf/Safe_and_Sound.pdf.

Clark, & Clark. (2004). Principal leadership for developing and sustaining highly successful middle level schools. *Middle School Journal, 36*(2), 49–55.

Clark, & Clark. (2006). Middle school leadership: What should accountability really mean to school leaders? *Middle School Journal, 37*(4), 52–58.

Cuban. (1998). How schools change reforms: Redefining reform success and failure. *Teachers College Record, 99*, 453–477.

Duckworth, Quinn, & Tsukayama. (2012). What No Child Left Behind leaves behind: The roles of IQ and self-control in predicting standardized achievement test scores and report card 29 grades. *Journal of Educational Psychology, 104*(2), 439–451.

Duckworth, & Seligman. (2005). Self-discipline out-does IQ in predicting academic performance of adolescents. *Psychological Science, 16*(12), 939–944.

Duckworth, & Yeager. (2015). Measurement matters: Assessing personal qualities other than cognitive ability for educational purposes. *Educational Researcher, 44*(4), 237–251.

Egley. (2005). Principals' inviting leadership behaviors in a time of test-based accountability. *Scholar-Practitioner Quarterly, 3*(1), 13–24.

Eid, & Diener. (2006). Introduction: The need for multimethod measurement in psychology. In *American Psychological Association handbook of multimethod measurement in psychology* (pp. 3–8). Washington, DC: American Psychological Association.

Fredricks, Blumenfeld, & Paris. (2004). School engagement: Potential of the concept, state of the evidence. *Review of Educational Research, 74*(1), 59–109.

Friedman, Kern, Hampson, & Duckworth. (2014). A new lifespan approach to conscientiousness and health: Combining the pieces of the causal puzzle. *Development and Psychology, 50*(5), 1377–1389.

Goldwyn. (2007). School leadership that works: From research to results. *Journal of Educational Administration, 45*(3), 340–342.

Hagger, Wood, Stiff, & Chatzisarantis. (2010). Ego depletion and the strength model of self-control: A meta-analysis. *Psychological Bulletin, 136*(4), 495–525.

Heckman, Strixrud, & Urzua. (2006). The effects of cognitive and noncognitive abilities on labor market outcomes and social behavior. *Journal of Labor Economics, 24*(3), 411–482. doi:10.3386/w12006.

Ireland, & Pennebaker. (2010). Language style matching in writing: Synchrony in essays, correspondence, and poetry. *Journal of Personality and Social Psychology, 99*, 549–571.

Jackson, & Lunenburg. (2010). School performance indicators, accountability ratings, and student achievement. *American Secondary Education, 39*(1), 27–44.

Jennings. (2010). School choice or schools' choice? Managing in an era of accountability. *Sociology of Education, 83*(3), 227–247.

Jones. (2005). The myths of data-driven schools. *Principal Leadership*, *6*(2), 37–39.

Kidd, Palmeri, & Aslin. (2013). Rational snacking: Young children's decision-making on the marshmallow task is moderated by beliefs about environmental reliability. *Cognition*, *126*(1), 109–114.

Kyllonen. (2012). The importance of higher education and the role of noncognitive attributes in college success. *Revista de Investigación Educacional Latinoamericana*, *49*(2), 84–100.

Lee, Lee, & Jang. (2015). How important are non-cognitive personality and personal background to the unemployment persistence in Korea? *Korea and the World Economy*, *16*(3), 345–377. Retrieved from http://www.akes.or.kr/akes/eng/publication/publication_07.asp?data_where=3.

Lewis. (2004). *Employee perspectives on implementation communication as predictors of perceptions of success and resistance.* University of Texas at Austin, Unpublished manuscript.

Lyons, & Algozzine. (2006). Perceptions of the impact of accountability on the role of principals. *Education Policy Analysis Archives*, *14*(16), 1–19.

Ransford. (2007). *The role of school and teacher characteristics on teacher burnout and implementation quality of social-emotional learning curriculum.* Pennsylvania State University, Unpublished manuscript.

Rosen, Glennie, Dalton, Lennon, & Bozick. (2010). No cognitive skills in the classroom: New perspectives on educational research. *RTI Press publication No. BK-0004-1009.*

Rothstein. (2014). *Accountability for noncognitive skills.* Alexandria, VA: AASA.

Rushton, Brainerd, & Pressley. (1983). Behavioral development and construct validity: The principle of aggregation. *Psychological Bulletin*, *94*(1), 18.

Schmidt, & Datnow. (2005). Teachers' sense-making about comprehensive school reform: The influence of emotions. *Teaching and Teacher Education*, *21*, 949–965.

Steinberg. (2014). What's holding back American teenagers? *Slate.* Retrieved from http://www.slate.com.

Szczesiul, Nehring, & Carey. (2015). Academic task demand in the 21st-century, high-stakes-accountability school: Mapping the journey from poor to excellent? *Leadership and Policy in Schools*, *14*(4), 460–489.

Tanner. (2014). The impact of No Child Left Behind on non-cognitive skills. Retrieved from https://sites.google.com/site/patrickseantanner/job-market-paper.

Tough. (2012). *How children succeed: Grit, curiosity, and the hidden power of character.* Boston, MA: Mariner Books and Houghton Mifflin Harcourt.

Uskali. (2004). What are schools to watch? Retrieved from http://www.schoolstowatch.org/what.htm.

Valentine, Clark, Hackmann, & Petzko. (2004). *Leadership for highly successful middle level schools: Vol. II. A national study of leadership in middle level schools.* Reston, VA: National Association of Secondary School Principals.

West. (2014). The limitation of self-report measures of non-cognitive skills. Retrieved from http://www.brookings.edu/research/papers/2014/12/18-chalkboard-non-cognitive%20west.

West. (2016). Should non-cognitive skills be included in school accountability systems? Preliminary evidence from California's CORE districts. *Evidence Speaks Reports, 1*(13), 1–7.

West, Kraft, Finn, Martin, Duckworth, Gabrieli, & Gabrieli. (2014). Promise and paradox: Measuring students' non-cognitive skills and the impact of schooling. Retrieved from http://cepr.harvard.edu/files/cepr/files/cepr-promise-paradox.pdf.

Chapter 5

The Use of SEL in the Classroom and Lessons for School Accountability

SEL must be prioritized to have a lasting effect in schools. Professional development of teachers is necessary to ensure SELs positive effects take root in the schools where it exists. Strong leadership is required for long-term success. Administrators and educators mostly agree that **SEL** assessments are needed for quality decision-making regarding the **SEL** presence in schools.

While **SEL** remains a controversial topic in testing and **school accountability**, it is increasingly important that it is sufficiently addressed in the academic setting. There are many changes to family structures, economics, and technology that contribute to socio-emotional issues in children (Goleman, 2005).

There is no one better to address these issues outside of the home than school-based educators as they have arguably the most significant contact time with youth outside of the family unit. One novel measure of whether **SEL** initiatives are implemented successfully is to include it in **school accountability**.

Nonetheless, because this is a new initiative, an understanding of educator and administrator experiences is key to knowing whether **SEL** does indeed belong in **school accountability**: Is it even possible to teach **SEL** skills and, moreover, adequately and fairly assess these "soft skills"? Only educators and administrators have the firsthand experiences to confirm whether this is true, yet one should consider that their opinions about such measures may be biased.

Many teachers experience the benefits of **SEL** in the classroom. They are able to connect their content areas to real-world examples, which helps them develop the students' content knowledge alongside embedded **SEL** opportunities. ESSA has certainly instigated the interest and perhaps the future necessity to assess **SEL** skills, identifying school systems responsible and accountable for developing the whole child (ASCD, 2011). Teaching students is not just geared toward the academic content but also toward developing them into whole people who can relate to one another positively.

People with high emotional intelligence have the ability to self-motivate, persist in the face of obstacles, regulate emotion, keep distress from hindering critical thinking, and empathize with others (Goleman, 2005). These abilities are extremely useful in all life situations.

THE CURRENT STATE OF SEL INSTRUCTION

It is more pressing than ever to teach **SEL** skills, especially because we now know from research that they can indeed be taught (Goleman, 2005). The W.T. Grant Foundation conducted a study of prevention programs and discovered that interventions were the most effective when they included the core of emotional and social competencies (Goleman, 2005). These competencies included impulse control, managing anger, and finding creative solutions to social predicaments.

Statistics demonstrate that students are worsening in the following areas over the last several decades: withdrawal or other social problems, anxiety and depression, attention and thinking problems, and delinquency or aggression (Goleman, 2005).

Intervention programs improve students with problems such as aggression and depression. The lesson learned from these programs is to generalize them as a measure for the entire school population but taught by teachers (Goleman, 2005). It is the school's responsibility to address these pertinent and disturbing issues, according to Goleman (2005).

Teachers who use emotional intelligence and social-emotional learning in their classroom insist that their students advocate for themselves in a positive way, learn in a positive environment, and support academic work. Having more student buy-in improves student academic achievement. There is an advantage for ELA teachers over other subject area teachers in regard to teaching **SEL** is that students are more revealing.

More humanities teachers are willing to teach **SEL** because they see the direct impact and benefit of teaching these skills to their students, and it is much more feasible for them to incorporate them into their subject area's curriculum authentically; moreover, teaching **SEL** also makes other subject areas, such as math, easier to teach, especially when students are motivated to take ownership of their work and learning as they see purpose for the work.

Knowledge of student profiles helps teacher's lesson plan and remediate when there are unexpected learning challenges. Goleman (2005) suggests blending lessons on feelings and relationships with academic topics.

Emotional lessons can integrate naturally into reading, writing, health, science, and social studies. In particular, **self-efficacy** is essential for the long-term success of students. **SEL** programs promote stronger academic work. There are many benefits to providing socio-emotional support. If **SEL** is taught correctly, students will not just improve their emotional intelligence, but their academic intelligence as well (Goleman, 2005).

These are skills that humans or people need to be functional and to interact with one another in a positive way, regardless of whatever setting one is in. Metamood is a term often used to suggest awareness of one's own emotions, whereas Goleman prefers the term "self awareness," the sense of an ongoing attention to one's internal states.

During this conscious attention, the mind observes and investigates experiences and emotions. **SEL** includes skills that educators are thoughtful when planning how they teach **SEL** skills, especially at the **high school** level because some teachers automatically jump to "well [the students] should know that by now," whether or not this is a realistic expectation to have of all students. **SEL** programs contribute to strong accomplishments in academic work.

Up to 50 percent of children demonstrate improved achievement scores and up to 38 percent have improved grade point averages (Goleman, 2005). Misbehavior also drops by 28 percent, suspensions by 44 percent, and other disciplinary actions by 27 percent (Goleman, 2005). These increases are truly remarkable for programs whose purpose is improved behavior.

Students are in crises now, and it is more vital to teach **SEL** skills, especially because they can indeed be taught and transfer across situations (Goleman, 2005). The teaching of impulse control, anger management, and discovering creative solutions ameliorate anxiety and depression (Goleman, 2005).

An improved socio-emotional state, therefore, clearly enables improved learning outcomes.

Some educators consider themselves content area experts and do not feel comfortable incorporating **SEL** into lesson plans especially because it was not provided within their teacher preparation programs. Unfortunately, many secondary teachers across the country do not receive **SEL** preparation because this is viewed as something that should be attained in elementary school. Elementary school teachers typically receive **SEL** preparation.

There is a need for **SEL** in all subjects, including difficult-to-teach subjects such as math. Even math teachers can use their content to deliver more connections through real-world examples and their own experiences. The hurdle arises with educators who are concerned that they themselves do not have the prerequisite skills to address socio-emotional problems in students' lives. Many educators who share this concern are already including **SEL** in their classroom at some level. They should be trained in understanding **SEL** so that they can leverage what they are already doing in their classrooms.

The majority of ELA teachers are generally interested in including **SEL** in their curriculum because they could see the direct impact that it had on their students who were already revealing themselves via their writing and analysis of written works. Support for **SEL** allowed humanities students to feel that their voices were being heard, and they were more likely to connect with the teacher and the subject. This connection motivated them intrinsically to learn more and to perform well, if not for themselves, then for their caring educator.

Negative outcomes are often blamed on teachers, not on students and parents. As a result, some teachers were very hesitant to support the addition of **SEL** to their curriculum because their workloads are already demanding. Teachers and administrators initially resisted the inclusion of **SEL** in accountability until they had more information. The lack of **SEL** assessment information was a detriment to their decision-making process regarding **SEL** inclusion in schools.

Successful school reform includes effectiveness, fidelity, and popularity (Cuban, 1998). **SEL** already has popularity within current education media sources. Its effectiveness is in the process of being determined; however, based upon this study, many educators and administrators see the importance of addressing **SEL** within **school accountability** because it has the ability to transform schools positively.

Regarding fidelity, the purpose of **SEL** from the CORE pilot program's prerogative is to improve academic achievement. CORE has run its own linear regression and found that **SEL** assessments have a positive impact on academic achievement (Bookman, 2015). This is proof that **SEL** meets the fidelity standard.

Educators are more likely now to question reforms and innovations. **SEL** is extremely popular in the education media with such outlets as *Education Week*. The perception among the media is that **SEL** is a valued change.

In terms of Cuban's (1998) popularity standard, **SEL** is very important. In terms of the longevity standard, it is too early to know for certain how **SEL** will perform in **school accountability**. More time is also needed to determine if **SEL** continues to provide the expected increased academic achievement which would signify meeting the effectiveness standard. The adaptability standard is subject to the time and resources of each school.

SEL programming fosters positive behaviors in students and improves motivation and peer relationships, which enhances the learning environment for all students. There are a wide variety of **SEL** programs that schools may implement to address a range of issues, such as conflict resolution and bullying. Teachers benefit from understanding where their students stand socially and emotionally; they may use **SEL** data to redirect their lessons for more meaningful engagement, which leads to improved learning outcomes.

RECOMMENDATIONS FOR SCHOOL LEADERS

Advice for superintendents is to provide district professional development to administration about **SEL**, **SEL** programs, and **SEL**'s stance within **school accountability**. Administration needs the right resources to provide to their staff.

These professional developments should include success stories from a current administrator, or someone that the current administrators could lean on for advice and suggestions on a regular basis. An assistant principal at all schools should be tasked with **SEL** inclusion within a culture and climate team or a separate committee such as a **SEL** advisory committee, which is often coupled with a PBIS committee.

Assistant principals need their own committees made up of other staff members including teachers and counselors. Administration could attend department staff meetings to address **SEL**. This would be particularly useful for the science and math teachers who have less exposure and understanding of **SEL** in the classroom.

It is also much easier to address **SEL** in smaller settings than in larger ones with all staff. More participants can ask the questions they need to be addressed which more directly impact their content area. Teachers would find it extremely beneficial to address **SEL** needs by content because each area varies greatly.

In addition to addressing **SEL** at specific content area staff meetings, separate trainings for science and math teachers would be extremely beneficial. Initial **SEL** trainings before **SEL** lesson plans are sent out would be the most beneficial.

It would be acceptable to combine social studies, humanities, world languages, art, and similar content area expertise teachers into a category for **SEL** trainings and then provide a separate **SEL** training for the computer science, science, and math-related disciplines. Finally, I would suggest that administrators observe classrooms for the sole purpose of examining the **SEL** usage within individual classroom settings; that way, they can have a more thorough understanding of its current usage by content area. A collaboratively derived look-for checklist could be implemented as a feedback and accountability tool.

Data drive districts and school efforts, resources, and time in a positive and meaningful way. Data aid in identifying the most effective learning environments for the classroom where success is evident. Most districts can use results to bolster student and school performance and change negative preconceived notions about school (Honig & Coburn, 2008).

Additional **SEL** research is necessary to determine its place within **school accountability** systems. Duckworth and Yeager (2015) argue that there is not enough research to support its inclusion in accountability due to validity concerns. Even though the **SEL** assessments may not be ideal or optimal in terms of measuring **SEL** without validity concerns, it is better to include them in **school accountability**, especially in a pilot program.

One can see the benefits in school culture transformation after its inclusion. More research is needed on **SEL** assessments generally and on pilot programs to determine if the weight of **SEL** assessments should be increased, decreased, or set aside altogether.

Perhaps, in time, a **SEL** assessment can be generated that is more objective and valid for **school accountability** purposes; meanwhile, schools would be worse off for ignoring **SEL** than for addressing it. In light of these recommendations, there are additional research questions that may fill the gaps in our current collective knowledge.

The following research questions suggest potential future research topics:

- What is the most effective approach to **SEL** training for educators, particularly subject-based educators who may have less interaction with **SEL**?
- How can administrators improve **SEL** engagement with all school staff?
- How can administrators motivate educators to view **SEL** data as more important?
- How may **SEL** assessments be developed to meet the needs of accountability?

These research questions were developed both to extend the current research questions and to fill gaps identified from available research and practices. Ignoring these types of questions at the school level may result in little regard for positive culture and climate building in schools, which is detrimental to the staff, students, our local communities, and society at large.

SEL must be purposeful with the community, school administration, and staff prioritizing it together for it to have the most positive effects. Student voice via surveys, committees, and other forms of feedback in particularly is vital for the continued improvement of **SEL** at the **high school** level, especially in fostering the student connection to the school. **SEL** data allows for more informed decisions to occur.

Professional development is particularly important for difficult subject areas such as math. It is the culture, purpose, priorities, and goals of administration which are the largest contributors to long-term **SEL** success at the school.

A strong leadership, collaborative culture which are set by the district and administrative leaders are essential for the long-term success of the school for which **SEL** is a large component. Although there were variations on perspectives of **SEL** in school accountability, the majority of teachers and administrators believe that the **SEL** assessments have a place in our schools.

Overall, most educators view **SEL** as beneficial, if not essential, to their students' education, even if it means increased workloads for them. Society has much gratitude for the work and service educators provide by striving to develop their students both academically and socially emotionally.

QUESTIONS FOR TEACHERS

1. How can educator experiences inform **SEL**'s usage in school accountability?
2. How can teachers who are hesitant about **SEL** feel more comfortable addressing it in the classroom?
3. How could humanities teachers aid in the professional development and collaboration of math and science teachers regarding **SEL**'s usage in the classroom?

QUESTIONS FOR SCHOOL LEADERS

1. How can administrators' experiences inform **SEL**'s usage in school accountability?
2. What kinds of training do teachers need to better understand **SEL** so that they may leverage its usage in the classroom?
3. Should the purpose of **SEL** be just improved academic achievement or something else?

ADDITIONAL RESOURCES

Safe and Civil Schools

Safe & Civil Schools is an improvement program for school climate and culture. The program uses a proactive, positive, and instructional approach developed and refined by Dr. Randy Sprick (2020). Professional development opportunities are available for both administrators and teachers across the United States and Canada.

The purpose of Safe & Civil Schools is to help adults create environments for children that are emotionally and physically safe. There are multiple volumes to the program that provide educators with sample discipline codes and guidelines for overall school improvement.

Permission to Feel: Unlocking the Power of Emotions to Help Our Kids, Ourselves, and Our Society Thrive

In this book, Brackett (2019) guides parents, educators, and everyone else on how to become an "emotion scientist." The author describes how society is unwilling to let people feel their emotions and what they are dealing with on a daily basis. This publication guides the reader through methods of understanding emotion regulation at various stages of life. Sufferers of their emotions are turning to unhealthy coping methods for stress reduction. Understanding one's emotions deters this unhealthy process and motivates one to learn new and healthier coping mechanisms.

ASCD. (2011). A whole child approach to education and the Common Core State Standards Initiative. Retrieved from http://www.ascd.org/ASCD/pdf/siteASCD/policy/CCSS-and-Whole-Child-one-pager.pdf.

Bookman, N. (2015, December 7). Personal interview.

Brackett. (2019). *Permission to feel: Unlocking the power of emotions to help our kids, ourselves, and our society thrive*. New York, NY: Celadon Books.

Cuban. (1998). How schools change reforms: Redefining reform success and failure. *Teachers College Record*, *99*, 453–477.

Duckworth, & Yeager. (2015). Measurement matters: Assessing personal qualities other than cognitive ability for educational purposes. *Educational Researcher*, *44*(4), 237–251.

Goleman. (2005). *Emotional intelligence*. New York, NY: Bantam Books.

Honig, & Coburn. (2008). Evidence-based decision making in school district central offices: Toward a policy and research agenda. *Educational Policy*, *22*(4), 578–608.

Spricks. (2020). About safe & civil schools. Retrieved from http://www.safeandcivilschools.com/aboutus/index.php.

Chapter 6

SEL Assessments for the Purposes of School Accountability

Schools were initially created to prepare students for jobs. That need changed over time for a need to prepare students for college as well. These continued types of changes in education require states and school districts to be flexible while keeping up with these ever-changing needs, which is challenging.

What is measured affects effective outcomes. If certain competencies like **SEL** are not held accountable, then they will less likely be taught in schools. There has been enough anecdotal and research evidence that demonstrates how **SEL** is needed for students' workplace successes.

THE PURPOSE OF ACCOUNTABILITY OFFICES

Depending on the size of the school district, a district may include a research, evaluation, and accountability department. These offices conduct strategic planning, continuous development through improvement plans, and specialized coaching for schools. They evaluate programs where are there are questions about the program's effectiveness.

Program evaluations help a school district where they are, where they need to improve, and what steps need to be taken to achieve positive change. Research interests are determined directly from identified district goals and initiatives. The accountability office provides suggestions on how to identify the root causes of problems and then creates action plans with schools to address outstanding issues.

The research and accountability offices conduct reports for the school district's board on such topics as discipline, World-Class Instructional Design and Assessment (WIDA) testing, immersion programs, **SEL** programs, and student homelessness (Melnick et al., 2017). For instance, they need to understand how formative assessments are measured. Data reporting and analyses, at the state and federal levels, are a response to the importance of accountability.

These offices are heavily affected by the NCLB era and are tied to data reporting, assessment, and state accountability systems. There is an idiom in the industry that "the accountability tail has wagged the education dog tail for too long" or vice versa (Page, 2020). The problem for educators is the call to "teach to the test." Educators are expected to make instructional decisions to placate the accountability machine. Nonetheless, this is slowly changing. School boards are using their research office's program evaluations to do less program cutting.

MATCHING THE DEVELOPMENT OF SEL ASSESSMENTS TO THE NEEDS OF ACCOUNTABILITY

Initially, **SEL** was viewed as a distraction from academics and poorly valued. Nonetheless, research has determined that **SEL** has a positive effect on school climate and on students' academic and later-life successes. **SEL** is a new opportunity for states and school districts to support their student populations through accountability systems.

Not all educators are trained in how to incorporate **SEL**, while many do not realize that they are already incorporating **SEL** skills into their daily interactions with students. **SEL** and positive school climate are essential for students' and staff's successes both at school and, in the case of the students, their careers. Because of this, states should be encouraging schools to support **SEL** in new accountability measures.

For instance, curriculum-embedded performance assessments, such as building a model with peers or conducting a research report, provide insight into students' academic skills in addition to their social-emotional skills, which range from **self-management** to collaboration. Due to this concept, New Hampshire is a forerunner state as it is investing in a performance assessment pilot in multiple districts.

These performance assessments would replace standardized tests with performance tasks. Some tasks include a rubric that evaluates students' **SEL** and their content mastery (Melnick et al., 2017). These rubrics are able to measure collaboration. While a student finishes a group project, the teacher and his or her student peers rate the student's cooperation capabilities or their ability to stay on task and focused.

Countries like Australia and Singapore that regularly use performance assessments in their examination systems require that students write in a daily research journal about what they accomplished as an individual and group member. This journal entry describes how they organized themselves, collaborated with others, withstood obstacles, and more. The journal entry is assessed along with the work product (Melnick et al., 2017). If journal articles such as this become a regular classroom practice, they can be used by the teacher to determine future student development and necessary support.

States could provide supports to school districts for new accountability measures through the usage of well-validated tools for the measurement of **SEL** and school climate. **SEL** measurements that are effectively designed and implemented may aid educators in making strategic decisions regarding needed investments in student services, programs, and professional development.

States that are not yet ready to use **SEL** and climate surveys may have them administered locally. The local administration of these surveys could serve as a model for a future state survey approach. There could be a set of survey options or a specific model of surveys for the state. States may offer school support via technical assistance. Tools could include protocols for teacher observations, reflections, and school practices. These can be found within the Classroom Assessment Scoring System (CLASS), a broader school quality review, or even a district-wide framework, such as the CASEL **SEL** rubric.

The most essential component is that measurements be locally relevant and easily accessible to school-wide decision-makers. School districts can experience school improvement due to the usage of **SEL**. The data are not enough to improve schools. Staff should receive training so that they can better understand what to do with the data they collect. That way, they can develop and administer high-quality programs and organizational changes to support student social-emotional development.

Not all states have this capacity, but organizations may provide technical assistance. Fortunately, ESSA provides multiple opportunities for funding school climate and supports for **SEL** including the Safe and Healthy Students block grants and school funding.

Continual research suggests that **SEL** has a positive school climate and the foundations for student success. Because of this, states should encourage schools to support **SEL** for the purposes of accountability and improvement under ESSA.

HOW CAN SCHOOL LEADERS IMPROVE SEL ENGAGEMENT WITH ALL STAFF?

School leaders cannot work in isolation. Successful leadership involves the entire community through consistent engagement. Roland Barth wrote, "Teachers have extraordinary leadership capabilities, and their leadership is a major untapped resource for improving our nation's schools" (Barth, 1990). Teachers are needed in the decision-making process. They are more inclined to sustain change when their voices are valued. They will be more consistent in ensuring policies are followed in classrooms, hallways, and schoolyards when they possess buy-in for an initiative they co-constructed alongside leadership.

If principals are willing to access the knowledge and skillsets of everyone in schools, they will create a successful, positive climate and culture. Schools have the potential to become places where students learn while feeling connected with adults. Adults in schools collaborate, and they create a sense of belonging, inclusiveness, vision, and practice. They need to share this collaborative spirit with their students, which furthermore models **SEL** coming to fruition in adulthood for the students whom they serve.

Shared leadership demonstrates that not just formal leaders have leadership prowess but that all school staff have this potential. School custodians may sense a student's connection to the school and may change that for the positive. Skilled principals nurture and capitalize on the leadership in everyone in the school community, making them better as a team than as individuals, which in turn creates a positive environment for both students and staff.

The strategy of involving all staff as leaders could be referred to as "Think Partnership." There is a balance of power in the view of leadership. All staff including teachers, parents, and students are partners. Principals know that these members need empowerment to ensure that all voices are heard and taken seriously.

This is especially important when implementing **SEL** in schools, so all parties know they have a stake in the ongoing implementation—**SEL** is a new endeavor that affects everyone. It is also important for everyone to sense that they are involved with **SEL**'s inclusion into school systems as all stakeholders have influence over it and should be unified in their efforts.

Once in alignment, all stakeholders will need to commit to shared responsibilities. Shared leadership works well when all parties share responsibility and accountability for the partnership work. Each stakeholder needs an active role and a roadmap for completing their responsibilities. The empowerment of teachers, staff, students, and parents to collaborate toward a common goal allows them to be cognizant of their role and others' influence.

Shared responsibility requires monitoring progress. Building respect and responsibility through shared leadership entails respect and responsibility when considering new ideas and strategies. All school stakeholders have their own skills and ideas on how to create a positive school culture. The partnership must recognize the differences in the group and celebrate them. Collaboration should foster respect and shared leadership to build a strong, cohesive team that works effectively together.

Shared leadership requires all stakeholders to have moral and performance character. Moral character involves ethical traits such as honesty and generosity. An approach that is fostered in shared leadership promotes students to rise up and become leaders themselves. Providing students opportunities to serve as leaders prepare them for the future because they already have the opportunity to exercise problem-solving skills with complex issues.

School climate problems are usually too immense and cumbersome for one person to address and change on their own. Teachers, staff, students, parents, and principals who collaborate are able to combat issues more collectively and powerfully.

Schools should develop leadership among various individuals who represent all types of stakeholders. A variety of models are needed to develop a school climate that engages adults and students in a shared mission with the purposes of improving student development at all levels, socially and academically.

Shared leadership can derive from principals and other administrators who are able to empower teachers to become leaders who will take responsibility for the schools' well-being (Barth, 1990). When principals demonstrate high expectations for students, parents, and teachers, staff can lead more effectively.

When all stakeholders lead together, they are better able to empower one another to effectively lead, engage, and meet the needs of all students. When this collective leadership does not occur, all parties are missing out on an important opportunity to improve schools, students, and the community.

Just as principals play a role in fostering a collaborative leadership style that involves multiple stakeholders, they also have a vital role in fostering a safe and supportive environment for teachers, parents, and students. Particularly when principals create new initiatives, it's important that they explain their vision to their staff and involve them in the decision-making process about the school.

The integration of **SEL** into the very makeup of the school allows schools to effectively and efficiently address students' social-emotional needs. This can be accomplished through classroom instruction and infusion into academic content, which follows PBIS guidelines. In order to accomplish this, all adults involved from leadership to support must understand the importance of **SEL** and how to best utilize it.

SEL is not always explicitly taught and often times is demonstrated through modeling behavior. First, the adults must have the social-emotional skills to regulate emotions, show empathy, and strive to meet challenges. Even school leaders may need to be developed before the students. When teachers and principals are socially and emotionally aware of how their emotions impact the classroom and the overall school environment, they are likely to support students in understanding their own emotions.

Adults who use **SEL** to help themselves are more likely to commit time and effort to promote **SEL** programs and practices that support students' **SEL** development. The creation of opportunities for teachers to engage in making decisions about **SEL**'s implementation in the school is an excellent way to have all staff on board and committed. Staff engagement will allow administration to obtain results the leadership wants. Unfortunately, the alternative is not acceptable; without educators and other staff support, the **SEL** resources allocated may be wasted.

Teachers need opportunities to learn about **SEL** through professional development trainings, colleague observations within their school or district, and conferences. Educators may become active and execute the collective leadership's decision to successfully implement **SEL**. Teachers are all coming into the profession with varying understandings of what **SEL** is and how it is operationalized. Leaders must recognize that **SEL** competence is ongoing and may take time in developing.

When principals are well trained in supporting **SEL** in schools, they are better able to drive positive staff culture and make **SEL** initiatives renewable through strong leadership and an effective allocation of resources. Principals should promote professional development on **SEL** that is explicit, sustained, and job embedded.

It is not only teachers but counselors and coaches among other related education professionals who benefit from training on how to teach social and emotional competencies and the best methods to infuse them into daily interactions with students. Effective training includes follow-up and opportunities for coaching that should ideally be differentiated based on the educator's experience, prior **SEL** exposure, and the needs of students being served.

Teachers who cooperate with others have a greater degree of experience with **SEL** implementation. They provide ongoing support to educators using **SEL** to improve their practice and to integrate the use of **SEL** assessments. These assessments can be used to make effective instructional decisions. Educators are in the need of sufficient time and training on how to understand the measurement tools being used to assess **SEL** before they are asked to respond to the data.

EFFECTIVE APPROACH TO SEL TRAINING FOR EDUCATORS

SEL has the ability to develop positive self-discipline approaches in students. In the past, punishments have been teacher focused and only temporarily forced students to behave ethically. The **SEL** approach is more prophylactic and permanent for behavior improvement. This is its major difference with PBIS and other classroom management approaches (Melnick & Martinez, 2019).

The **SEL** approach is strong in developing social and emotional competencies in self-discipline and preventing behavior problems. Where **SEL** is not as effective as in the correction of behavior problems, that is where a different approach like PBIS is helpful (Melnick & Martinez, 2019). A common mistake that educators make in regard to self-discipline is the belief that by preventing and correcting behavior, they are creating self-discipline.

Although the PBIS and **SEL** approaches are similar, they are also different in important ways. Together they provide a full range of strategies and techniques for effective classroom management and school-wide discipline (Melnick & Martinez, 2019).

Data can be an effective driver for decision-making when school districts allow them to be such. Data are able to provide pressure and support for improved leadership at the school level. Both administrators and teachers make evidence-based decisions. Unfortunately, the data can often be anecdotal from the perspectives of school staff (Bear, 2010).

There is a current focus on academic performance data to guide school improvement. Accountability-driven reform efforts assume that the greater the attention that is given to collecting school data, the more student academic performance will improve (Bear, 2010). Nonetheless, evidence to support this claim is not substantial.

Few principals consider anything but test scores as a data source. For instance, more principals could use teacher performance from formal or informal observations to guide improvement goals and progress. They could also consider individual or group professional development plans.

Principals and teachers should develop teacher capacity to engage collectively in data analysis for instructional decision-making. This process can be associated with professional learning community initiatives which are paid for by the school district.

Principals play a key leadership role in setting the purposes and expectations for data usage by providing structured opportunities for data-use training and assistance. Access to expertise through effective training and setting up follow-up actions are keys to success (Bear, 2010). Teachers often times value training completed by other teachers or those who were teachers. Educators consistently consider trainings conducted by fellow educators to be the most effective and practical. There is an increased level of respect for those who have practiced the craft of teaching. They are coming from a place of authority on the subject.

Teachers do not consider data implications on their own; they need a school leader to guide them in this endeavor. Principals often times use the orientations and expectations they gather from the central office. If the district is not using data for educational decisions and school improvement, then data use does not occur at the school level.

A positive correlation between district data-use and academic achievement occurs when principals believe they have the ability to meet the district's improvement goals. The data is only useful when principals have the ability to meet improvement goals set by the district. The district's role should be to provide pressure and support for initiatives that they can improve. Unfortunately, data usage that does not increase capacity can have a negative impact.

Schools have the ability to influence teaching and learning in positive ways through the support of principals. With increased student poverty and diversity, the principals decrease their shared and instructional leadership with the teachers.

Teachers in lower-income and higher diversity schools report that they are less likely to see teacher leadership and shared responsibility for student learning (Bear, 2010). Therefore, both principal and teacher leadership for improving student learning decreases as poverty and diversity also increase.

Teacher and principal leadership decrease as poverty and diversity increase in both urban and rural-urban areas. Additionally, these schools struggle to develop strong shared leadership with parents. Student poverty and district size create an enormous disadvantage. Large districts with a high-poverty student population are more likely to have limited leadership, even when controlling for school level, size, and urban location.

Teachers are more likely to distrust their principals in middle and **high schools**. They are less likely to report that their principals are actively involving parents and teachers in decision-making. Middle school and **high school** teachers tend to believe that their principals are not instructional leaders in the building (Bear, 2010).

High schools have a greater "leadership deficit" than middle schools. There is a gap in this type of leadership which is needed for states and districts as they take increasing responsibility for improving educational outcomes.

Both principals and teachers must feel successful and efficient in their work. While school districts are able to influence teaching and learning through positive feelings of efficacy is on the part of the principals (Wahlstrom et al., 2010).

Efficacy is one's belief that the accomplishment of goals and tasks as possible. The concept was developed by Bandura. Efficacy beliefs affect the choices people make about the types of activities to engage in and how they can cope with efforts once the activities begin (Bandura, 1997). With stronger feelings of efficacy, there is more persistence and how much effort people will expend and how long they will persist in the face of challenge.

It is principals who have strong efficacy beliefs who are more likely to undertake and persist in school-improvement projects. There are two types of efficacy, individual and collective. Individual efficacy propagates the sense that the individual has the ability to accomplish a task or goal.

Collective teacher efficacy (CTE), a theory generated by John Hattie, refers to when a group possesses the shared belief that it has the ability to accomplish a task or goal together. CTE is the collective believe of school staff to positively affect students. This positive collective belief improves student academic achievement. A school staff that believes in its ability to accomplish greatness is vital to school health. When there is a collective believe that positive outcomes are possible, then it is more likely to occur.

It is a principal's tendency toward a collective efficacy that is a key to their leadership style having influence over teaching and learning. Personal and school characteristics have the potential to affect principal efficacy. Some examples of school leadership to incorporate **SEL** into their schools include the following (Wahlstrom et al., 2010):

- All adults ranging from leadership to support staff must understand the importance of **SEL** and how to support it. **SEL** is not accomplished through discrete lessons but can be used as a method to further develop students.
- All adults should receive **SEL** training. When teachers and principals are aware of their own emotions and how they impact the classroom and overall school environment, they are more likely to support students in understanding their own emotions.
- Generate opportunities for buy-in and teacher engagement about **SEL** decision-making and implementation. Educators are an essential component of any **SEL** initiative. Without their buy-in, **SEL** resources may be wasted.

Educators must have the ability to observe their peers at their school or within their district, attend conferences, and participate in decision-making about how **SEL** is implemented at their school.
- Create **SEL** professional development that is detailed, job related, and sustainable. Follow-up and coaching are essential components for educator learning which is tailored based upon experience and prior **SEL** exposure and the needs of the student population.
- Supporting educators through the use of **SEL** assessment for instructional purposes. These assessments may provide impactful data about students' **SEL** competencies, which teachers may use to enhance instruction. Educators need enough time and training to understand the measurement tool and how it relates to the school's **SEL** implementation framework before being asked to use the data.

HELPING EDUCATORS TO VIEW SEL DATA AS IMPORTANT

First, administrators need teachers to enter the classroom ready to teach **SEL** and understand the significance of **SEL** data. Collaboration among teacher preparation programs, districts, and schools have the ability to best prepare teachers to support students' social and emotional development across instruction.

States should promote the competencies teachers need to foster students' **SEL** in state teaching standards. A strong emphasis on **SEL** in teacher licensing and accreditation could help bring commonality to how **SEL** is taught (Melnick & Martinez, 2019). It may also create the expectation that all teachers need to meet these standards.

States and teacher programs may adopt performance assessments that request teacher candidates demonstrate proficiency in **SEL** competencies as a requirement for teacher licensure.

One state that is taking steps to address this need is California where new Teaching Performance Expectations include **SEL** standards, culturally responsive teaching, and the ability to provide safe learning environments (Melnick & Martinez, 2019). Other states may supplement their current teacher candidate assessments to ensure that candidates can demonstrate the needed skills to support students' social-emotional well-being.

Federal, state, and local levels can invest in university-district partnerships that enhance teacher candidates' field experiences and the districts' ability to support students' **SEL**. Teacher candidates need strong mentor teachers who are able to effectively address **SEL** dynamics of teaching and learning. Incentives for these partnerships can be supported by states and districts through funding and technical assistance.

Multiple-tiered efforts can support school and district leaders' learning about **SEL** and their administrators' role in supporting teachers and students. If principal and district leaders set **SEL** as a priority, then it will remain one. High-quality principal development requires funding.

States should use federal funds to supplement the expenses of principal preparation programs. States may wish to take advantage of targeted funds such as Title II in ESSA to make strategic investments in their school leader workforce (Melnick & Martinez, 2019).

Resources and technical assistance can help schools and their district advance **SEL** for staff and students. It is up to policymakers to make these resources available. Educators need training to determine schools' needs for high-quality programs, professional development, and school organizational changes that support students' development. Some school districts in California for instance already have the professional development support from multiple sources, but unfortunately not all schools and districts know where to receive this help.

Such support can include technical assistance, peer learning networks, and funding to improve schools' means in supporting students' **SEL** (Melnick & Martinez, 2019). States and districts are able to furnish well-validated tools to measure **SEL**, school climate, and other school supports.

Schools currently need well-designed and well-implemented measurement tools so that educators can make strategic decisions about necessary resources for student services and programs. These services and programs can range from measures of **SEL** and school climate to diagnostic measures including observation and reflection protocols to enhance educator practices. In addition, staff surveys can strengthen educators' voice in their own professional development and allow them to suggest which supports they need the most (Melnick & Martinez, 2019).

To create a strong classroom culture, the Center for Reaching and Teaching the Whole Child (CRTWC) suggests creating classroom norms together at the beginning of the year (Melnick & Martinez, 2019). This enables teachers to encourage engagement through culture-building activities and to address classroom issues that disrupt equitable student participation.

Growth mindset is not only important for students but for educators as well. A **growth mindset** empowers learning, whether that is learning new content in school or learning how to be an effective instructor. Fixed mindsets lead to disengagement from difficult tasks.

There are methods within literacy instruction where teacher candidates may foster the development of a **growth mindset** and that is through guided reading. Literacy Professor Jolynn Asato suggests guided reading or the practice of having students read leveled books for their reading level under the guidance of a teacher (Melnick & Martinez, 2019). The teacher uses a writing workshop where he or she models for students the various stages in the writing process.

CASEL and other similar organizations provide helpful lessons on various approaches to developing and measuring **SEL** skills at local levels. CASEL disseminates practitioner guides for **SEL** programs for pre-K through grade 12 (Melnick & Martinez, 2019). Participation in working groups which facilitate the collaboration of leading researchers and school districts in establishing practical **SEL** measures.

Although principals may believe in **SEL**'s potential to facilitate success for their students, some are less enthusiastic about its potential for higher academic achievement. They are more convinced of its potential to help students improve school climate, citizenship, and relationships than academic achievement (Melnick et al., 2017).

Even though principals understand the importance of assessing students' **SEL** competencies, they do not have enough experience with the tools to do so. Knowledge should be shared on existing measures so that researchers, funders, and policymakers prioritize improving **SEL** assessments.

One of the greatest potentials in understanding **SEL** exists in building an understanding of how to appropriately use **SEL** assessments and the data they produce (Melnick et al., 2017). These data have the potential to increase all student **SEL** competencies and evaluate the effectiveness of **SEL** programming implementation.

Principals understand how vital **SEL** is to student development and their successes in and out of school. Students need guidance and support to make effective school-wide implementation a reality. Principals understand that **SEL** competencies are teachable and that they should be developed in all students. Students equipped with **SEL** competencies become better students and then improved adults.

The modern world is filled with increasing and demanding work along with the dissolution of American communities. It is necessary to foster, instruct, and model self-awareness, **social awareness**, **self-management**, relationship skills, and responsible decision-making (DePaoli et al., 2017). These competencies are the ones that hold society together with a robust economy and vibrant democracy.

SEL improves student academic achievement; however, more proof of these impacts is needed for action to occur. Even though principal support for **SEL** in culture and classrooms is significant, the various types of **SEL** implementation vary widely across schools. One in three principals promotes a school-wide **SEL** program, and only one in four meet benchmarks for high-quality implementation (DePaoli et al., 2017).

When principals and teachers who attempt **SEL** are supported by their district leadership, they have improved student outcomes. As state policymakers support their district leadership, the outcomes are even more apparent.

There are factors that may slow **SEL** implementation at the school and district levels. Although there is strong support for **SEL** among principals and teachers, they need support, resources, and tools for effective **SEL** implementation (DePaoli et al., 2017). In this way, they can ameliorate students' attitudes toward learning as well as their CCR.

Teachers enter the profession with a variety of **SEL** interpretations. Educator development with **SEL** competence is continuous and time-consuming. Teachers develop their **SEL** practices while they collaborate with their colleagues (Melnick & Martinez, 2019). They use **SEL** data for instructional decision-making with the purposes of nurturing students' **SEL** and academics (Melnick & Martinez, 2019). For instance, teachers express concern over whether or not **SEL** assessments are distinguishing anxiety.

Teachers may add a valuable perspective on student **SEL** development. They sometimes have an insight into what students themselves cannot see such as their levels of **social awareness** and responsible decision-making. Such tools range from surveys to observations of performance on tasks accompanied by a scoring rubric (Melnick & Martinez, 2019).

According to a study conducted by Harvard University, researchers who found that there is moderate to strong correlation between student and teacher **SEL** assessments (Melnick & Martinez, 2019). They suggested that such assessments may provide correlative information about student's **SEL** skills that could inform school and grade level planning for curriculum development.

Teacher surveys or observations are the most common measure of **SEL** in younger students. Educators evaluate students in the early grades on social interactions and **self-management** which is conducted through surveys. Certain surveys are created for special services while others are strengths based which uses age appropriate and maladaptive behavior. These may provide useful information about students.

A widely used survey tool is the Devereux Students Strengths Assessment (DESSA) where teachers report the extent to which students demonstrate certain competencies (Melnick & Martinez, 2019). The DESSA-Mini is a shortened eight-question survey for diagnostics; it serves as a time-effective tool for teachers to monitor progress.

In some school districts and states, teachers are asked to evaluate students' **SEL** skills on report cards as a means to foster a dialogue among students and their families pertaining to the students' development.

Students' **SEL** competencies may provide useful information for districts and schools to positively influence their practice at the school. **SEL** assessments that evaluate habits and mindsets may guide students' personal strengths and growth potentials. Student surveys that are controlled for the classroom, school or district may inform potential areas for improvement (Melnick & Martinez, 2019). This data could impact program, curriculum, and training investments.

When assessments are administered over time, these assessments may determine if the various types of initiatives piloted to ameliorate students' **SEL** are working which promotes more drive school-level decision-making (Melnick & Martinez, 2019). A district or school could use these data to assess areas where multiple schools are struggling. Various methods such as student observation, computer-based tools, student-, peer-, and teacher feedback may be influential tools at the classroom level (Melnick & Martinez, 2019). These data permit staff to tailor **SEL** to their instruction.

SEL data may encourage reflection and open conversations among teachers, students, and parents about the competencies that students should learn in the future. When there is daily feedback and reflection, there is an ongoing focus for **SEL**. If **SEL** assessments are implemented at the local level, teachers must be resourced to use effective strategies to generate student learning and growth. While some **SEL** interventions have a proven track record, there is not always a clear path for educators to know how to best help students develop skills such as grit (Melnick & Martinez, 2019).

Not providing teachers the needed resources for **SEL** intervention may be counterintuitive. According to mindset researcher Dweck (2006), more research is needed before teachers create their own interventions.

THE NEED FOR SEL

In today's home environments, parents have less opportunities to teach their children the social-emotional skills for success. There are many families who have other commitments, and they can no longer meet the social-emotional needs of their children. Not every child is taught **SEL** at home. These children only have the opportunity to acquire these needed competencies at school, but those only if their school is teaching them. Teachers are obligated to teach these skills so that they are successful in the classroom because they are held accountable for the content knowledge which cannot be acquired without **SEL**.

There are many changing shifts in education. At first, there were no public schools, and as a society, we understood the dangers of not providing equal access to free K-12 education. Just as desegregation happened, Title 9 for gender equality, and changing religious education to a classical education occurred, there is a new upward trend in education that must be addressed in order for equity to really be attainable (Melnick et al., 2017). **SEL** is similar to all these previous needed changes. We are holding back certain students because of their inability to learn **SEL** at home.

Schools were originally meant to just prepare students for jobs. Education had to change its focus to also include college preparation. Nonetheless, educators made a concerted focus to address this change. Education has evolved significantly over time, and it has evolved with changing times and needs to best serve the public.

If education's purpose is to prepare students to be productive in society, then **SEL** skills must be measured in schools. From a teacher's perspective, there is the need for **SEL** in the classroom. Unfortunately, what is not assessed is less likely to be taught. Measurement equates to effective outcomes.

Many researchers and entrepreneurs discuss the need for soft skills to be ready for the workplace. Collaboration, empathy, and decision-making skills are some of the most important skills for contributing to success in the workplace (Melnick et al., 2017). If **SEL** is not taught to students, then we are not preparing them for that future.

QUESTIONS FOR TEACHERS

1. How can PBIS guidelines aid in the development of **SEL** in students?
2. How can observing other teachers help educators align **SEL** to their content?
3. What kinds of support do teachers need from **SEL** coaches?

QUESTIONS FOR SCHOOL LEADERS

1. How can school administrators leverage teacher leadership when developing effective **SEL** tools for their schools?
2. How can administrators obtain the buy-in from all stakeholders regarding **SEL**'s usage in schools?
3. How can administrators empower families to take leadership roles in addressing a school's **SEL** needs?

ADDITIONAL RESOURCE

Preparing Teachers to Support Social and Emotional Learning

This report informs policymakers, practitioners, and teacher educators about the components of purposeful **SEL**-focused teacher preparation and development programs (Melnick & Martinez, 2019). This study offers information on how pre-service and in-service teacher training supports best teaching practices and integrates **SEL** in schools. The report provides information on routine **SEL** uses in the classroom (Melnick & Martinez, 2019).

Bandura. (1997). *Self-efficacy: The exercise of control*. New York, NY: Freeman.

Barth. (1990). *Improving schools from within: Teachers, parents, and principals can make the difference*. San Francisco: Jossey-Bass.

Bear. (2010). *School discipline and self-discipline: A practical guide to promoting prosocial student behavior*. New York: The Guilford Press.

DePaoli, Atwell, & Bridgeland. (2017). *Ready to lead: A national principal survey on how social and emotional learning can prepare children and transform schools. A report for CASEL*. Retrieved from Washington, DC.

Dweck. (2006). *Mindset: The new psychology of success*. New York: Random House.

Melnick, Cook-Harvey, & Darling-Hammond. (2017). *Encouraging social and emotional learning in the context of new accountability*. Palo Alto, CA: Learning Policy Institute.

Melnick, & Martinez. (2019). *Preparing teachers to support social and emotional learning: A case study of San Jose University and Lakewood Elementary School*. San Palto, CA: Learning Policy Institute.

Page, C. (2020, February 10). Personal interview.

Wahlstrom, Louis, Leithwood, & Anderson. (2010). *Investigating the links to improved student learning: Executive summary of research findings*. University of Minnesota: The Wallace Foundation.

Chapter 7

SEL's Ability to Bridge the Learning Gap

This section addresses **SEL**'s ability to bridge the learning gap through teacher-led role modeling, teacher training, and **SEL**'s ability to address many types of learners. Teachers must model appropriate emotional intelligence behaviors for their students to be successful in **SEL**. For this to occur, teachers need **SEL** training to effectively produce **SEL** lessons. **SEL** can provide the necessary supports for a variety of learners including special needs students and speakers of other languages.

When teachers have respectful relationships with students, they are able to more easily have respectful relationships with parents and the community. This mutual respect fosters informed decision-making among everyone. In turn, students develop basic competencies and work habits for meaningful employment. Relationships with students are key to keeping students engaged and motivated.

Teacher behaviors create more positivity in the classroom by allowing students to stay on task, help one another, and transition from one activity to another seamlessly (Schonert-Reichl, 2017). When teachers do not have **SEL** competencies, classrooms are more likely to be unruly, disruptive, and unfocused. Teachers must maintain a high social-emotional competence themselves in order to spark and maintain a high level of student **SEL** in the daily classroom.

It is easier to address **SEL** in English classes than in science and math classes. Nonetheless, teachers have the ability to relate, teach, and model **SEL** for their students. If a teacher has strong **SEL** and is able to relate more readily with students, he or she is able to reach more students effectively, no matter the content area. All teachers can engage and interact with students in pro-social ways.

In the mathematics classroom, it is true that there will be awkward moments at first when establishing an **SEL** routine and culture (Jones et al., 2009). If students are accustomed to traditional classrooms, they will not be accustomed to addressing active listening and conflict resolution in a math class (Jones et al., 2009). However, with concentrated practice, both the teacher and the students will come to understand the **SEL** expectations in this context (Ee et al., 2014).

MOST EFFECTIVE SEL TRAINING FOR EDUCATORS

An effective understanding of **SEL** allows educators to overcome burnout, efficiently manage their classroom, and, most importantly, maintain positive relationships with their students. Managing stress properly for teachers is more important than ever.

According to the MetLife Survey of the American Teacher, teachers are stressed at unprecedented levels (Jones et al., 2013). Principals are also experiencing more stress and job dissatisfaction than ever before. This stress trickles down to the students who have negative views of their school environments with other negative factors increasing, such as bullying, mental health problems, and peer pressure.

Teachers should receive emotions-focused training. Emotional regulation may help teachers deal with stress and such challenges as the emotional burden of student trauma. Just like the students, teachers need to reflect on their emotions and what causes them. They need to reframe, problem solve, and manage their emotions to make them easier to handle. For instance, there is a two-day training for the Recognizing, Understanding, Labeling, Expressing, and Regulating (RULER) approach, which has been deemed highly effective for teachers and students (Jones et al., 2013). Teachers can receive additional training on how to relate **SEL** to their content areas. They are eligible for up to five coaching visits in their classrooms.

The RULER approach is an **SEL** program that provides suggestions for class charters called RULER charters which aid with classroom norming at the beginning of the year. Chapter 8 will contain further details about classroom contracts and their utility. These types of charters can also be helpful for making home-school connections and for team-building exercise for administrators.

An example of a RULER charter in the classroom is: How do you want to feel? What will you do to feel that way? What do we do when we do not feel that way? These questions guide the discussion and the creation of the class charter. The teacher can pass around an object such as a school mascot object around the classroom, so each time the person holds the object, they are the speaker. There can be a recorder who jots down what is discussed so that the teacher can facilitate the official class charter at the end of the discussion.

An example of a family charter to promote a home-school connection is as follows: As a family we want to feel . . . . In order to have these feelings, we will . . . , and we will manage (and prevent) conflict by . . . . This family charter can be created through a survey to parents and then disseminated through a class newsletter, Google Classroom, Edmodo, ClassDojo, or Remind.

Other potential forms of **SEL** professional development sources for educators include other **SEL** programs such as 4Rs (Reading, Writing, Respect, Resolution) + MTP (My Teaching Partner) (Jones et al., 2013). This program provides classroom-based feedback and suggestions for educator improvement; it is essentially **SEL** coaching. The program provides educators with the necessary skills to use **SEL** in the classroom on a daily basis while integrating **SEL** practices naturally into their content areas. This program benefits both teachers and students because they simultaneously develop **SEL** skills.

MTP maintains training videos on their website (Jones et al., 2013). They also implement one-on-one coaching bi-weekly for teachers. Through this program, teachers upload videos of their **SEL** lessons. Observations and feedback are provided through a Classroom Assessment Scoring System, which emphasizes student-teacher relationships and interactions (Jones et al., 2013).

Another helpful training method to provide educators is mindfulness training. Mindfulness can be taught via breathing, reflection, meditation, and yoga. This approach is centered around a state of being. Mindful people are focused and aware of their surroundings. They are nonjudgmental and accepting of a variety of very difficult situations. Essentially, they are more adept at handling changing pressures and anxiety than unmindful people.

Given the modern challenges in teaching today, mindfulness practices are extremely beneficial and important. Students and teachers need this approach when they have a quiet moment or if they require a walk around the school to find a moment of peace to center and reflect upon their emotions. Mindfulness helps all professionals become less reactive and more reflective, responsive, and flexible to challenges.

Two mindfulness programs exist that could be extremely beneficial for educators. They include CARE (Cultivating Awareness and Resilience in Education) and SMART (Stress Management and Resiliency Training) (Jones et al., 2013). Both of these programs' purpose is to encourage teachers' mindfulness, relationships with students, job satisfaction, and efficient emotional regulation. Emotional regulation is extremely important because it provides both students and teachers the ability to reflect upon challenges and learn from them in positive ways which lead to more connection to the school and job satisfaction.

Not unlike students, teachers may benefit from structures and routines which remind and guide them in the usage of **SEL** competencies. Such routines may include calming-down techniques, breathing exercises, and affirmations. Some **SEL** programs promote the usage of these techniques through poster reminders.

One way to make these strategies effective is to constantly remind students of their usage, just like teachers educate their students to raise their hands or form lines. **SEL** techniques, then, are just as much a part of classroom routines and cultures as the existing, everyday classroom expectations and norms.

SEL competencies must be included in daily school life for everyone including students, teachers, staff, and administrators. They are necessary for everyday interactions among everyone for positive outcomes to occur at all levels. This transition may be difficult for many school systems, especially because they are so focused on academic achievement. Nonetheless, **SEL** has the potential to positively influence student academic achievement in new ways.

The inclusion of **SEL** at a school-wide level signifies that the administration and staff must build emotional awareness together. They should understand how their emotions affect instruction and student learning. This could be addressed in staff meetings and professional development trainings. It may also be explored through journal, blogs, and videotape reviews.

While some educators may resist discussing emotions, school leaders will need strategies for increasing their emotional awareness, nonetheless.

Strategies would need to include ones that address teacher backgrounds, personalities, and cultures. Some strategies may need to be indirect. For instance, when teachers reflect on how students perceive them as educators, they can develop their emotional awareness through the activity.

Addressing students' **SEL** needs in the classroom is a critical task for teachers so that they may build student trust and respect (Inlay, 2016). Students attempt to belong, feel connected to their peers, and discover who they are and what they would like to become (Inlay, 2016). Creating a culture of respect starts with the individual and then manifests itself through their behaviors.

Teachers can build a culture of respect by building student capacity. They can do this by fulfilling students' social-emotional needs. When teachers help fulfill students' **SEL** needs, they are more likely to experience a sense of belonging and connection to the school, which ultimately achieves a sense of identity and self. They can also model for students the respect they would like to see in their students (Inlay, 2016).

When students feel they are a part of a group, they feel better about their relationships and about themselves. Then they are more self-confident. With this confidence, they are more likely to respect others because they respect themselves (Inlay, 2016). The work of attaining a respectful classroom must begin with the students' attitudes and beliefs, which then moves outward toward behaviors (Inlay, 2016).

Teachers should listen to students deeply, and not just to the words, but to the overall message or purpose of what the students are communicating (Inlay, 2016). Teachers should also take student ideas seriously and treat them with profound respect (Inlay, 2016). Dismissing student ideas is disrespectful, and students will not easily forget the lack of respect which makes them less likely to pay attention in the class or feel compelled to complete the work. In other words, students work harder and learn more when they feel connected to and respected by their teachers.

Educators can support their students by addressing their ideas critically in a discussion or assignments. This is because students are capable of creating solutions to problems and to monitor themselves. Engagement is facilitated by their own intrinsic motivation.

Student idea requests offer teachers the opportunity to teach about leadership, organizing a solution, and facilitating conflict resolution, commitments, and consequences (Inlay, 2016). The creation of a discipline system where the primary goal is teaching important lessons about respecting oneself as well as others promotes the **SEL** skills for success in students.

Teachers who connect with their students fulfill their sense of belonging and identity, which leads to respect for others (Inlay, 2016). The encouragement of students to take responsibility for their own actions is vital for their own personal development.

Educators should not blame themselves but reclaim their power that they have the ability to choose their own attitudes when it comes to student interactions (Inlay, 2016). The ability for teachers to communicate their own mistakes with their students is a model behavior which demonstrates the need to take responsibility for one's own actions.

Reflection should be included in daily practice. Reflection is the process of understanding what is occurring, why, and how it must be changed. It is an essential competency for reacting efficiently in difficult circumstances (Jones et al., 2013). This process should be regularly modeled and reinforced.

Administrators can incorporate reflection into meetings and supervision. One way of doing this is the pros and cons list at the end of the meeting, where the team facilitators ask the team participators for what went well and what did not during the meeting. This reflection process informs future meetings on the part of the meeting organizers.

Furthermore, reflection can be built into meetings through colleagues being assigned partners or teams for regular reflective discussions. All staff can be encouraged to take regular time for reflection, even if it is just five minutes at the beginning of the day and five minutes at the end. Staff should habitually ask their staff about personal and work stress and work with them to reduce stressors like scheduling and providing tips for stress relief (Jones et al., 2013). Such tips can be taking deep breaths, meditating, and talking about frustration with colleagues. They should also provide referrals for mental health services when needed.

Administrators can create a culture of continuous improvement and learning. Nonevaluative supervision, open staff discussions, and open-door policies can motivate staff to be reflective and knowledgeable about **SEL** competencies, which are also personal strengths that need improvement. An emotionally safe learning environment is essential for exploring these subjects.

Integrating adult **SEL** with ongoing approaches to address student **SEL** entails a significant shift in what we consider to be the purpose of education (Jones et al., 2013). Social and emotional competencies are not secondary to the main purpose of education. Instead, they are tangible success determinants for teachers, students, and schools.

The more teachers use **SEL**, the more the students will as well. Successful student learning is dependent upon a teacher's ability to manage the class as a whole by keeping their attention and redirecting negative and distracting behaviors (Jones et al., 2014). Teachers need knowledge of student behavior to optimize student motivation and engagement.

Classroom management is rarely developed in teachers adequately enough during teacher preparation programs and professional development training to yield substantially effective practices. Therefore, teachers seldom feel that their classroom management is a match for their students. The strategies suggested in **SEL** programs can provide teachers the needed ones to have effective classroom management (Jones et al., 2014).

Classroom management is not about demanding perfect student behavior. It is about supporting students to manage their own emotions, expectations, and reactions (Jones et al., 2014). Students necessitate the tools from the teacher to provide them with their needs to effectively meet the demands of an **SEL** school environment.

Teachers find it difficult to deal with interruptions because students do not understand how to regulate their emotions (Lopes et al., 2012). Emotion regulation has been ignored in education until recently. Students need to balance academic learning and growth. Learning emotional regulation is one of the best methods to improve academic growth.

Emotions influence the way in which students think and behave. Teachers have the ability to guide attention, facilitate learning, and coordinate student interactions through tangible emotion regulation strategies. Intrapersonal and interpersonal emotional regulation is linked because emotions are contagious in that students can "catch" the emotions of others, according to Lopes et al. (2012), in a process called co-regulation. Essentially, mirror neurons prompt others to take on the emotions of others around them.

Effective classroom management is based on planning and preparation. Teachers need a sense of where **SEL** can fit in while lesson planning, and they need strategies to address problems as they arise in a positive manner.

Some example **SEL** strategies for managing classrooms include using rewards as motivators for good work and behavior. These rewards may include PBIS certificates/awards, calls/emails home, homework passes, or treats such as candy and school supplies. Other strategies include using a visual board to show where centers or review stations are located, encouraging students to talk about their feelings, especially when they need an ear, and the use of nonverbal hand signals without interrupting instruction for questions such as a request to use the restroom, get water, or go to the nurse.

SEL helps teachers respond to student behavior in new ways. **SEL** programs focus on supporting the development of children's executive functions and regulatory skills. It aims to build teacher skills via improved instructional practices, warmth, and awareness (Jones et al., 2014). The ultimate goal of any effective **SEL** program is to develop communities of self-regulated learners.

THE ENGAGEMENT OF A VARIETY OF LEARNERS

Many types of learners—whether they are on individual education plans (IEPs), 504 plans, ESOL services, heritage speakers, or other types of learners—need support to succeed in school. Students with disabilities in particular need **SEL** to address the complex environments of schools and how their interactions in this environment may lead to different outcomes and even stigma (Elias, 2004).

There is a section in IEPs that make various suggestions on how to address social and behavioral support for these students. One such suggestion includes student encouragement to ask for assistance when needed. Other suggestions include the need for self-regulating strategies to address when responding to peers in a manner that is not expected.

A student with an IEP needs an adult to prompt or remind the student how to respond to peers in these situations. Furthermore, the reinforcement of positive behavior through nonverbal/verbal communication helps these students because students with IEPs are motivated by positive reinforcements. These students' teachers should provide positive reinforcement on a daily basis with a varying level of appropriate intensity.

Some students with IEPs require a social/academic performance daily report to increase parent/school communication. These students struggle with focusing attentiveness, and they need effective strategies to overcome this challenge. Frequent teacher checks for understanding will allow the student the opportunity to keep up with instruction.

Teachers should communicate missing assignments with the parents in writing or over the phone. If possible, all students should be given the opportunity to make up missing assignments for the quarter once the parents have been contacted. Note-taking during instruction may aid these students in reviewing the material after the class which will help increase the students' learning of the content and therefore improve course grades.

The method to address students with IEPs is very similar to the way in which teachers should address students with 504 plans. These students often need extra time, additional explanations, and graphic organizers to successfully complete the work. Regular check-ins with these students are essential. Just like the students with IEPs, a daily progress report may be sent home for the parents to see how the student is working in class, whether they are prepared for learning, and if they are behaving expectedly.

The following strategies are helpful for learners who are ESOL in all classes. Teachers should have extra activities planned in case they run out of activities during the class period. Ready-made activities that are **SEL** focused but still promote the use of academic language are especially helpful if an activity does not work as expected, the students are not understanding, or technology fails.

It is essential to plan carefully and realistically about what the students can accomplish, given their levels. It is best to divide activities into shorter increments, such as fifteen minutes. Placing a timer on the board also helps students keep track of their own efforts. Students who are ESOL need partners to help them understand the content when it is unclear.

Heritage speakers in world language courses are extremely beneficial for all learners in the class. Their modeling of correct pronunciation, new vocabulary, accents, and cultural knowledge is invaluable to other types of learners in the classroom. Teachers should encourage them to correct others and provide feedback. Nonetheless, it is important to note that heritage speakers must be aware that they need to be kind and supportive of others whose first language does not happen to be the target language. Nobody likes to feel made fun of or laughed at in class, so it is important that a culture of acceptance is explained and expected from the beginning of the year.

When disrespect occurs, the heritage speakers should be addressed. An effective call-out phrase for world language classes is to state in the target language, "If you cannot make a mistake." And the students respond, "You cannot do anything."

World language students in particular must know it is important to at least try to speak in the target language because if they do not, they will never succeed in learning any part of the language. Making mistakes while students live in an English-speaking country is easier than entering the country of destination where the target language is spoken and making incomprehensible mistakes then.

To conclude, teachers model positive behaviors for their students to emulate. It is easier to teach **SEL** in language classes than science and math classes because of the flexibility in the content delivery. **SEL** training for educators is a necessity because of the continued job stress.

Teachers need **SEL** coaching so that they may see positive models that utilize **SEL**. They must be shown how to use it effectively, too, just like their students need this type of modeling. **SEL** techniques such as encouraging students to take responsibility for their own actions are highly effective. Teachers should reclaim their power by demonstrating these qualities and skills.

It is equally important to provide IEP students with the accommodations they need to succeed. ESOL students need supports in strategies and tools to achieve success. **SEL** can provide the necessary supports for all learners, but especially those that necessitate additional supports.

QUESTIONS FOR TEACHERS TO CONSIDER

1. How can teachers help students manage their emotions, expectations, and reactions?
2. What kinds of tools can teachers provide students to improve their **SEL** competencies?
3. How can teachers make stronger home-school connections with parents through **SEL**?

QUESTIONS FOR SCHOOL LEADERS TO CONSIDER

1. How can administrators find the best **SEL** program for their school and students?

2. How should administrators provide effective nonevaluative feedback for their teachers so that they may improve their **SEL** practice in the classroom?
3. What are the most effective ways to provide **SEL** coaching for teachers in the classroom?

ADDITIONAL RESOURCE

Promoting Social and Emotional Learning: Guidelines for Educators

The book provides principles for serving schools, families, and communities facing challenges which can be best served by **SEL** (Elias et al., 1997). The authors reference scientific studies, theories, and site visits to describe approaches for **SEL** learning at all levels. There are sample guidelines, examples, programs, approaches, and ideas for schools, districts, and classrooms to follow.

Ee, Mingming, & Wong. (2014). Teachers' infusion of social emotional learning. *Journal of Teaching and Teacher Education, 2*(1), 27–45.

Elias. (2004). The connection between social-emotional learning and learning disabilities: Implications for intervention. *Learning Disability Quarterly, 27*(1), 53–63. doi:10.2307/1593632.

Elias, Zins, Weissberg, Frey, Greenberg, Haynes, . . . Schriver. (1997). *Promoting social and emotional learning: Guidelines for Educators.* Alexandria, VA: ASCD.

Inlay. (2016). Creating a culture of respect through the implicit curriculum. *Middle School Journal, 47*(2), 23–31.

Jones, Bailey, & Jacob. (2014). Social-emotional learning is essential to classroom management. *The Phi Delta Kappan, 96*(2), 19–24.

Jones, Bouffard, & Weissbour. (2013). Educators' social and emotional skills vital to learning. *The Phi Delta Kappan, 94*(8), 62–65.

Jones, Jones, & Vermette. (2009). Using social and emotional learning to foster academic achievement in secondary mathematics. *American Secondary Education, 37*(3), 4–9.

Lopes, Mestre, Guil, Kremenitzer, & Salovey. (2012). The role of knowledge and skills for managing emotions in adaption to school: Social behavior and misconduct in the classroom. *American Educational Research Journal, 49*(4), 710–742.

Schonert-Reichl. (2017). Social and emotional learning and teachers. *The Future of Children, 27*(1), 137–155.

Chapter 8

Strategies on Creating an SEL Environment in World Languages

In this section, we explore how and why educators must set high expectations from the beginning of the year is presented. The need for class contracts or charters is an effective practice that can aid in setting classroom norms at the beginning of the year which last all year long. Teachers can repeat their expectations and classroom contracts or charters as frequently as they need. Furthermore, students necessitate group work for developing collaboration skills. Lastly, teachers can use student feedback about their content and **SEL** delivery to improve their instruction.

Teachers should expect students to rise to meet high expectations from the beginning of the year and express this expectation all year long, so that they live up to those standards. Setting norms at the beginning of the year is vital for success all year long. One way to accomplish this is through a class contract or agreed upon class rules at the beginning of the year, which helps tremendously to set the tone for an effective year of learning, success, and joy. These class contract or class rules are created together first by giving an example of the school rules and creating the class version together and agreeing upon them.

The setup of the class contract can be done in the target language in advanced classes. Everyone should sign the contract, including the teacher, who should also check that all the students sign it. Holding them accountable by asking them to sign it if they do not is a must for everyone to feel obligated to abide by the democratically chosen rules. If they do not sign it, they feel that they have leverage to not adhere to the agreements, which reduces the overall morale of the entire group.

After winter break, if morale is low, this is an excellent time to review the class contract, which can be done through various engaging activities, such as verbal quizzing with prizes. Often, breaks are not an enjoyable or fun time of year for students who experience or have experienced trauma. Teachers can ask classes what can be done when students feel sad after horrific events, such as a relative dying, fighting in school, or if they are suicidal. Teachers and students support each other from the beginning in case these issues come up during the year.

Teachers can assign students to write an essay in English or in the target language in advanced world language classes as another effective way to determine and define norms at the beginning of the school year. In the essay, students can express want they would like the teacher to know about them, what they want to learn, and their expectations for the course. The students reread the essays throughout the year to see if expectations are being met.

A class discussion on whether or not the expectations are being met is a conducive way for both the teacher and student to reflect on their practices and modify their choices, or even the expectations themselves.

Fostering relationships among students and between the teacher and students is extremely important for establishing a comfortable class culture. Group work and partner work foster those relationships in class. If someone does not have a partner, the teacher assigns them one or a group, so no one is left out. Occasional teacher participation in the activity with the students models appropriate behavior and learning.

COMMUNICATION WITH WORLD LANGUAGE STUDENTS

The objective of each lesson should be written clearly on the blackboard for each class and is communicated to the class at the beginning of each lesson. Teachers should verify with students to ensure that the objectives and lesson activities are understood. Students are also encouraged to help one another when they do not understand.

Teachers can provide instructions on what is about to be covered in the class, and the directions can be repeated. Teachers should ask the students if they needed clarification before continuing and pause long enough for students to be able to respond. Students can also "turn and talk" about their understanding of the class objective while the teacher monitors for engagement and listens in to some of the conversations; utilizing input from this, teachers are more apt to clarify any misunderstandings or lingering questions.

While the students start the warm-up, the teacher should walk around the room to clarify any additional questions. If a particular question is asked several times, then the teacher should make an announcement to the whole class because other students may have the same question and are just hesitant to ask.

All lessons should follow the curriculum framework, so it is clear where each lesson is headed. Students should not be not confused or question why we are studying a particular subject. They should know where the class is headed because of messages on boards, Google Classroom, and teacher instructions. This makes it easier for students to understand their expectations social-emotionally as well.

If a lesson is a discussion, they need to participate and be polite. If a lesson is more individual based, they know that they should work quietly, and if a lesson is group or partner work based, they should collaborate.

Students need a synopsis at the beginning of class what they will be doing throughout the class, so that they know what to expect. A timer should be used and posted on the board through such sites as www.classroomscreen.com, and the teacher should ask the class if they need more time, especially if the lesson permits it. The teacher may build in extra time and have extra activities planned in case there is extra time. It is never beneficial for the students to be left to their own devices because they will find something to do. Such practices lower the affective filter and, therefore, assist with a focus on learning instead of anxiety.

Every class has a different rhythm, so it is best to match the task of transition to the particular temperament of the class. Some classes require attention be received more often, especially in larger and early level courses. To capture the attention of a class, the usage of callouts, countdowns, and clapping to get their attention are effective social-emotional tools to use that are consistent and positive.

A timer also serves as a reminder to students that they are transitioning onto the next activity, and it demonstrates how much time they have to generally accomplish a task. Nonetheless, students who need more time should be given and not rushed.

If a student particularly struggles, allowing them to take the work home is an excellent means of allowing them to finish on time. This flexibility regarding the students' ability to complete tasks within the original timeframe demonstrates to the students that the teachers care about their ability to complete the task given. This practice shows the students that the teacher cares about their aptitude for comprehending the task, completing it the best they can, and collaborating with others who may need help.

REVIEW IS ESSENTIAL FOR SUCCESS

Another method for retaining classroom culture is constant review of material and classroom norms set up at the beginning of the year. The review of norms in a particular **SEL** approach that is essential for effective classroom management and a positive learning environment.

Providing plenty of time to review also helps build student confidence in the content. Review activities may include jotting down what vocabulary words they can remember per each category we have studied, such as food, conjugations, telling time, numbers, seasons, and so on. Station reviews where students move around to various stations in groups focusing on topics that they have recently studied.

SEEK FEEDBACK FROM STUDENTS

At the midpoint of the year, such as after winter break, is a formidable time for students to complete a goal-setting task for the new year and provide feedback about instruction. Below are potential questions to ask classes:

- Do you feel that the goals for learning are clearly communicated to you?
- Do you know the purpose of our lessons?
- Are procedures and instruction easily understood?
- Is new instruction connected to prior lessons?

INCREASE STUDENT ENGAGEMENT

Students need a variety of activities to keep engaged and comfortable in a positive **SEL** environment. Providing multiple explanations in a variety of ways reaches the most students possible. Students need examples of other students' work to understand how to complete an assignment, especially if it is ambiguous at first. Hand gestures and callouts captivate and grab their attention. Interactive games like charades, Pictionary, card games, hangman, and bingo keep them engaged and on task. Students also enjoy online games such as kahoot, quizziz, and quizlet live.

In the advanced classes, they can lead classes through presentations on a relevant topic, within the curriculum, which builds effective communication and leadership skills. Students can create an online game for the class to participate in at the end of the presentation to help maintain class engagement. As a means of motivating participation, homework passes can be given to the winners as a reward.

These students who are leading the class create a student-centered learning environment. Although these motivators are extrinsic in nature, these opportunities allow students to celebrate learning in positive ways and feel recognized and valued by their teacher.

Students need constant feedback which should be both written and in person for them to more effectively grow their learning. Teaching strong study and organizational skills helps tremendously. For instance, flashcards for verb conjugations in a language class may help them learn verbs for tests. Having them present in the target language with puppets also helps. When students have these skills, they are prepared for success and less likely to feel anxious about their learning and scholastic achievement.

When students are about to go on vacation or are just returning from vacation are excellent times to do more relaxed activities with is showing **SEL** awareness as the teacher. Students are not in a headspace to perform difficult tasks at these times, and it is important for teachers to recognize that and not force challenging tasks.

For instance, students can practice animal names, and when they return from a break, they discuss what they did during vacation doing a puppet show. They can introduce the animal name in the target language like M. Le Chien (Mr. Dog). They are practicing salutations, animals, greetings, and vacation vocabulary.

A critical aspect of a positive **SEL** classroom environment is student voice. Every student should feel comfortable sharing their voice at any part of a lesson, where it is appropriate. One method to accomplish cohesive student voice is to provide each student with three Popsicle sticks and return a Popsicle stick each time they share their voice. Teachers should encourage all students to use them and not let a student use more than three. This process creates equity in the classroom.

In terms of **SEL** learning, achieving equity is essential for student buy-in. If students do not feel that their teachers value their voice, they are less likely to feel a connection to the learning. Then they are also less likely to participate in learning and collaboration, which is the purpose of using **SEL** practices.

MAKING CONNECTIONS ACROSS CULTURES

Culturally responsive teaching (CRT) is an engagement strategy to motivate students who are both culturally and linguistically diverse (Hammond, 2015). Students are more likely to engage if teachers reference their own heritage's history and culture in their teaching. Teachers can foster a considerable connection between brain-based learning and rigorous CRT (Hammond, 2015).

The ability to make cultural connections has the potential to close achievement gaps. There are brain-based principles that encompass CRT. Teachers can aid students in using their natural abilities, cultures, and languages to thrive in the classroom.

Making connections across cultures allows **SEL** competencies to flourish in the classroom. Some examples of making connections across cultures in a world language class include Spanish speakers appreciating the connection to their language. Additionally, francophone Africans appreciate more rigor in a French class such as silent reading, debates, presentations about a variety of subjects including music, innovation, scientists, elections, and holiday celebrations in their home countries within the target language.

Relevant celebrations of learning motivate students to feel engaged with the content. Such celebrations include guest speakers from home countries, field trips to embassies or to cultural organizations such as the Alliance Française, and celebrations of learning where they make crêpes or beignets for Mardi Gras.

CONNECTING THE LANGUAGE WITH CULTURE AND SEL

Every culture differs and matters when you teach a world language. Language is a part of culture. World language teachers must keep in mind how to phrase new concepts, how to use nonverbal gestures, and how to permit and omit certain details when using the target language as much as possible with gestures and translation. It is best to omit anything students have difficulty understanding at their level of the language.

Light-hearted expressions keep the environment upbeat and **SEL** focused. They allow students to feel socially connected. The inclusion of funny expressions that are commonly said in the target language such as "Oh là là!" encourage students to remember it and repeat it during the year. If someone swears, consistently stating something like "language scolaire" or scholarly language encourages them to keep each other accountable as well.

QUESTIONING AND DISCUSSION TECHNIQUES

Students need activities that will allow them to effectively practice their self-awareness and **social awareness**. Such activities could include warm-ups in world language where students can discuss an article, poem, or song. An example of such an article can be about the climate change agreement in Paris. Student volunteers could be asked to read the article aloud. The teacher can ask the students to consider the purpose of the agreement and write a paragraph in their journals about it.

This lesson would be rigorous because students continued to learn new concepts and utilize knowledge they had previously learned in terms of vocabulary and continued to learn new relevant terminology to the topic of climate change and science. Furthermore, the lesson is a **SEL** and humanitarian issue in its own right. Utilizing **SEL**, teachers do not have to shy away from deep assignments that imply harsh consequences for humanity if changes do not occur.

Responsible decision-making is extremely important when discussing issues that require critical thinking skills. Higher-order thinking questions such as "What will result now that the United States does not adopt the climate change agreement?" "What expectations are there of the United States now from other countries?" These questions are level 2 comprehension questions in Bloom's Taxonomy. Bloom's Taxonomy is a set of three hierarchical models used to categorize educational learning objectives into levels of complexity and specificity.

In this context, students can be asked to promote a deeper understanding of the issues that they are addressing. Students could be asked to think about these questions when writing their interpretation of the article in their journals for reflection.

With each discussion point, if there was a way to push forward student thinking, a teacher could assist by asking them "Why is that so?" and "Can you explain your statement further?" These questions are examples of the Depth of Knowledge (DOK). DOK is a scale used to gauge the amount of thinking necessary for a teacher-directed question or task.

Teachers who align questions to different DOK levels promote higher-order thinking and deeper learning for their students. There are four levels to the scale, depending on the difficulty of the task. Using the DOK stem questions from level 2 such as "support ideas with details and examples," "describe the features of a place or people," and "identify and summarize the major events in a narrative" encourage independent and critical thinking. The DOK model is useful for promoting student facilitated learning which further promotes **SEL** in the classroom.

During discussions, students have opportunities to create questions for both the teacher and the class that are analytical and detailed. These questions are task dependent after they have addressed the text-dependent questions. These level 3 stem questions delve deeper into their critical thinking by asking them to provide additional examples and the features of the problem. It is difficult in a world language class to reach a level 4 question because of the level of French language for the students.

These best practices in instruction yield a positive **SEL** environment. To ensure that all students participate in the discussion, referencing the seating chart and check off when a student participated. This also holds the teacher accountable for encouraging a variety of speakers. If a student does not participate on their own, then calling out their name and asking if they have anything to add to the discussion may increase engagement.

Students are motivated to create their own questions and participate because of an emphasis on collaboration or participation points. Students can be encouraged to ask the presenters their own questions as well.

The best situation is to facilitate student learning where the students are leading the discussion themselves. When this occurs, they are taking on a role that will allow them to improve their own social-emotional competencies by serving as a role model and demonstrating effective **SEL** competencies such as **social awareness** and responsible decision-making. Encouraging students to ask their own questions at the end of their presentations and selecting who in the class will respond to those questions is an excellent opportunity for developmental growth.

It is essential for teachers to set high expectations from the beginning of the year for students to follow throughout the year. These expectations can be referenced whenever necessary. The use of a class charter or contract facilitates classroom norming. Students may occasionally need brain breaks to more effectively contribute to group work and to their own individual work. Group and partner work can be improved through turn-talk exercises. A timer keeps classes on track and extra time can lower student anxiety, when needed.

Callouts, countdowns, and claps are examples of acceptable social-emotional ways to capture student attention. An effective professional development tool for teachers is to seek direct feedback from students to see how they are grasping the content. This student feedback can also be used to discover the effective social-emotional aspects of the class and what could change to better reach their students's social-emotional needs.

Some students necessitate a variety of explanations in order to reach the optimal number of students. Online games and other rewards keep students engaged. Best practices include the usage of Bloom's Taxonomy and DOK questions which challenges students and keeps their interest.

QUESTIONS FOR EDUCATORS

1. How can teachers create a comfortable class culture?
2. How can teachers best foster positive relationships with their students?
3. How can CRT help teachers address diverse learners?

QUESTIONS FOR SCHOOL LEADERS

1. How can administrators support teachers in addressing diverse learner needs?

2. How can administrators provide insightful feedback to teachers about their questioning techniques that encompass their **SEL** needs as well as their content needs?
3. How can administrators provide feedback that would help teachers engage their students using **SEL** competencies?

ADDITIONAL RESOURCE

Culturally Responsive Teaching and the Brain

CRT is a motivational tool to reach diverse students of various backgrounds (Hammond, 2015). Teaching culture and ways to address differences in culture can be a mysterious process for some teachers in comparison to other instructional practices (Hammond, 2015). This book provides helpful methods and suggestions for addressing diverse learners in the classroom.

Hammond. (2015). *Culturally responsive teaching and the brain: Promoting authentic engagement and rigor among culturally and linguistically diverse students.* Thousand Oaks, CA: Corwin.

Chapter 9

Language and Culture's Effects on SEL in the United States

Communication is key in a world language classroom. Our thoughts and methods for communication change based upon which language we are speaking. Bilingual and multilingual students have worldview perspectives that differ from their monolingual peers. These perspectives improve the ability to understand multiple personalities and situations with more complexity. Conflict arises in each language and culture differently. The ability to understand multiple languages and perspectives aids in conflict resolution.

In distance learning formats, communication is a challenge for students who are unaccustomed to working online. Many questions about access to textbooks, technology, and understanding the content occur on a daily basis which can be overwhelming for educators who are also unaccustomed to the change to the learning environment.

THE NEED FOR INTERCULTURAL SENSITIVITY IN THE CLASSROOM

Anthropologists define culture in a variety of ways (Lazear, 1999). These ways include shared morals, beliefs, expectations, traditions, expressions, and ceremonies (Lazear, 1999). Language is the way of connecting all these aspects together. Societies share many cultures and languages. While the majority of Americans speak English, a significant population of U.S. inhabitants speaks Spanish. There are even a variety of accents, vocabulary, and idioms among various regions of the United States within American English (Lazear, 1999).

This combination of interconnected cultures in the United States instigated a tolerance not seen during any other time of American history. Multiculturalism or the societal tolerance of many different cultures and languages seems to have increased in the United States (Lazear, 1999).

There has been a growth in bilingual education because of a demand in need. Previously, many immigrants insisted that their children learn English so that they could become Americans. The notion of multiculturalism has changed that tendency. In 1900, 85 percent of all immigrants in the United States were fluent in English (Lazear, 1999). That changed from 2009 to 2013 where the fluency rate dropped to 79 percent despite improvements in communication (U.S. Census Bureau, 2015).

The origin of language occurred initially because of thought (Sarles, 1976). Language is a system of thought about human nature and reality. Language enables communication, society, and culture (Sarles, 1976). Humans develop consciousness through understanding others and how others understand them. The consciousness of the "I" allows for the consciousness of the "you" (Sarles, 1976). Therefore, language is a social process and construct.

The overall purpose of language is social action. Grammar organizes social interaction because politeness, identity, and presentation of oneself is a major use of language (Atkinson, 2002). Language helps us maintain relationships with people while we present and perform our own identities and roles (Atkinson, 2002).

Noam Chomsky started an important discussion in the 1960s about how language defines our understanding of concepts. Chomsky suggests that language creates the parameters around what we can think. He found that one thinks within the bounds of language, and in that way, language controls what we are able to think.

If our language does not allow a particular construct in our native language, it is difficult to do so in another language. This process confirms that one's thoughts exist in the confines of language. For instance, grammatical principles are abstract. Learners of a particular language systematically make one set of errors but not another (Newmeyer, 1987).

Our perception of reality is influenced by the language we speak. Language literally shapes our thoughts. Our cultural perception changes our notions of time management, the appropriate role of **self-efficacy**, and motivation among other social-emotional constructs.

Just as **SEL** helps students improve their academic performance and testing performance, so does world language. There are many cognitive benefits to students from learning world languages which include improved IQ tests and a more positive attitude toward the target language (Tochon, 2009). Noncognitive benefits or **SEL** benefits include understanding relationships, responsible decision-making, and **social awareness** in a variety of cultures and languages.

Students who learn world languages develop a wider worldview. They are better able to understand different traditions, behaviors, customs, and values (Tochon, 2009). They build upon their tolerance of differences including combating racism. The knowledge of more than one language strengthens student self-esteem and identity. These attributes are social-emotional in nature, so in effect, students who are versatile in other languages are more socially and emotionally aware.

In the world language classroom, the importance of intercultural awareness is more apparent than in other subjects. Students are encouraged to explore what it means to exist in a third space between language and culture (Scott et al., 2013). There has been a recent shift from the study of monolinguals learning a new language to the study of children from diverse linguistic backgrounds and how they learn a new language (Garcia, 1993). This is because there are many more of these types of learners in the United States. World language instruction has needed to shift to address these new learners.

Studying a world language can offer insights into what it means to be a citizen in the present day. Students who are ESOL are able to express a new understanding clearly and succinctly in the context of being a global citizen (Scott et al., 2013).

The world language curriculum is uniquely situated for fostering awareness about the ways in which language learning promotes students' emerging identities as members of a global community. Relativizing self and valuing others are at the heart of what world language teachers do (Scott et al., 2013). Students learn effective **self-management** strategies in that they must think more slowly and critically in order to deliver more accurate language. World languages further develop self-awareness in students as well as they are learning to be patient with their learning process.

An intercultural sensitivity is fostered in students proficient in world languages other than English. They are able to build trust more effectively and make more substantial decisions. They have an improved grammatical understanding of their native language which allows them to write and speak with increased precision (Tochon, 2009).

This process builds confidence in students which can also help them become more socially aware. While learning a world language with other peers, students who excel in the process are more willing to help others who are struggling with languages, whether it is their native language or another.

Furthermore, world language students demonstrate greater creativity and adaptability because of their tolerance of different worldviews and lifestyles (Tochon, 2009). They are better able to understand one's own culture because they have another culture for which to make a comparison. Multilingual students are also more likely to be accepted by colleges and universities than their monolingual peers. This adaptability transfers over to the workplace in that they are more willing to collaborate and be flexible with others.

HOW SEL SITUATES ITSELF ACROSS CULTURES

SEL has called attention to the need for the teaching of emotional regulation in schools. The key to all learning is the quality of relationships and when hearts are touched where genuine community is thriving. All cultures address the teaching of **SEL** differently. There are different approaches to addressing emotions in education both in the United States and abroad (Hoffman, 2009).

A culture includes the shared norms and values of a group of people (Duckworth, 2016). All **SEL** skills including responsible **self-management**, responsible decision-making, relationship skills, self-awareness, and **social awareness** can differ across varying cultures. **SEL** is bound within a cultural context. One example pertains to time management which falls under **self-management**. For an individual, whether teacher or student: What does time mean? What does it mean to manage it? What are the cultural expectations for time, and how do these expectations communicate trust, respect, and social values?

Different cultures perceive, treat, and use time differently; it could be incredibly difficult to have a uniform application of time management as a **SEL** skill for an entire class. Each classroom could represent thirty different cultures or more. Even within the same culture, the individual interpretation of time varies within the culture.

For instance, in some cultures, it is perfectly normal to come an hour late to an event. While in other cultures, it is considered extremely rude. Explaining cultural expectations to teachers and students is critical to avoid discrepancies in outcomes. While in most school settings all over the world, the expectation is that both students and teachers be in the classroom on time, there are reasons why a student could be late such as a doctor's appointment, finishing a test in another class, or speaking to the main office about attendance.

Exceptions to being in class by the start of the class period can be made when students present a pass which is a formal excuse. Teachers should not be critical of students who are legitimately tardy or absent.

Nonetheless, students will take advantage of situations and show up to class habitually late because they are conversing in the hallways with their peers. When teachers explain the loss of education, their lack of preparedness for instruction and the class, and the overall distraction to the other students in the class, it provides them with the "compelling why" that they need to be successful in the class.

Responsible decision-making can vary significantly in that each culture makes decisions differently. Some cultures value group decisions more than individual ones. There may be cultural expectations in some households that require that students sacrifice their own personal successes in school in order to meet family goals.

These personal sacrifices are demonstrated through effective relationship skills and **social awareness**. The students naturally understand that they must make certain personal sacrifices for the overall well-being of their families. They understand that there are grave consequences for not making such sacrifices.

Some cultures do not allow their children to use birth control. Based upon their own cultural norms, these parents do not let young people decide if they should take it for medical purposes and not reproductive ones.

The implications for the students are that they do not feel that they have the ability to make responsible decisions on their own, which may impede their social and emotional development and confidence in the future. As educators, it is helpful to understand the effect that families have upon their children's decisions because it may impact their ability to focus and learn in the classroom.

Coming into a classroom as a teacher, it is essential to understand that these varying cultural norms may contradict the ones that they are accustomed to, and they have to become flexible in their dealings and responses to their students in order to be socially-emotionally responsive.

While some cultures may expect their children to have strong relationship skills with their peers and other community members, other cultures may value individual gains and a lack of interaction with their communities to meet their personal success goals. Coming into a classroom with students' varying perceptions of successful relationships can be taxing when attempting to create a strong **SEL** environment among diverse cultural expectations and norms.

An open mind is needed to engage students who are introverted, extroverted, and everything in between. However, knowing that students may be impacted by their cultural upbringing is helpful when addressing the integration of these differing cultural expectations, norms, and deep-seated ways of being.

It is important to know upfront that not every student is going to find someone to work with and that the teacher may need to help them find their group or partner. Giving the students time to find their own groups is beneficial. It is equally important to let the students know that if they do not have a group or partner, once the time is up for finding one that the teacher will choose one for them. This motivates students to find their niche, and if they cannot, the teacher can help assign them to a group or partner that will fit with their personalities, strengths, and weaknesses.

Group/partner projects and activities help students understand the importance of collaborating with others in the real world, whether that is within their communities, workplaces, or families. Some students may distrust this type of learning activity, but it is a necessary part of the **SEL** process that students learn to compromise, lead, support, and collaborate with their peers.

Self-awareness, a component of **SEL**, is simply an awareness of one's personality or individuality. It should not be confused with consciousness. While consciousness is the state of awareness of surroundings, body, and lifestyle, self-awareness is the recognition of that awareness. Goleman (2005) describes **self-efficacy** as the belief that one has mastery over events of one's life and can meet challenges as they come up.

According to Goleman (2005), emotional self-awareness includes the following qualities: the improvement in understanding and identifying one's own emotions, the ability to comprehend the source of feelings, and the ability to distinguish between feelings and actions.

The ability to manage emotions is related to self-awareness. Examples of the ability to manage emotions include improved frustration tolerance and anger management; fewer verbal insults, fights, and classroom disruptions; the ability to express anger appropriately, without fighting; fewer suspensions and expulsions; less aggressive or self-destructive behavior; and more positive feelings about self, school, and family (Goleman, 2005).

Culture, preference, and personality may change students' self-awareness. For instance, some students may be more inclined to accomplish difficult tasks in the morning. This tendency can also be influenced by culture.

In some societies, a long lunch is needed in the afternoon, where everyone enjoys a break for two hours; they either go home or go out to lunch so that they decompress. Then, they return to work and school. If students are coming from a culture that assumes this norm, and it is embedded into their everyday routine, it is extremely difficult to adapt to a culture where society takes a half-hour break at most and resumes work promptly.

Teachers can think of ways to approach this cultural difference by giving students the opportunities for brain breaks. There can be a station in the classroom with a box of activities that they can do such as listening to a relaxing music app, taking a walking break pass, or booklet or app they scan of beautiful images. A brain break tells students that it is acceptable to check-out in a positive social-emotional way that is not necessarily academic. It is not healthy for anyone to constantly feel pressured to accomplish work because the work quality may be worse without a brain break.

Students can use a wheel of awareness tool to discern their ability to focus their awareness. The wheel of awareness includes quadrants labeled as follows: interior of body, first five senses, mental activity, and interconnection. There are descriptors along with the wheel that encompass each quadrant.

When students are stuck on one particular point in their wheel of awareness, they can be helped by an adult, either a teacher or parent. An adult can help them decide where to focus their attention, so they can gain more control over how they feel (Siegel, 2012). This can be done by simply telling students that their feelings arrive and pass. They should begin to understand that these are temporary states and not permanent traits (Siegel, 2012).

Students may need help understanding their sensations, images, feelings, and thoughts. Mindfulness activities can help children to calm themselves and focus their attention where they would like (Siegel, 2012).

Social awareness is related to relationship skills: it is the process of understanding how interactions with others may influence relationships. Goleman (2005) describes the handling of relationships as the ability to analyze and understand relationships. In his definition, the following attributes are essential to handle relationships effectively and have adaptive **social awareness**:

- The ability to resolve conflicts and negotiate disagreements
- The ability to solve problems in relationships
- The ability to be assertive and skilled in communications
- Friendly and involved with peers
- Sought out by peers
- More concerned and considerate
- More pro-social and harmonious in groups, more sharing and cooperation and
- More democratic in helping others

Students need ways to capitalize on how the brain conducts social interaction. Everyone needs positive mental models for relationships. By creating these positive models, teachers and students need to enjoy time spent together through positive and satisfying experiences with the people they are with the most (Siegel, 2012). This is especially true when students are from various cultures. They need to see positive role models in the target culture so that they understand how to cooperate best with others.

Connections should be made through conflict. Conflicts do not need to be avoided but are viewed as an opportunity for learning essential relationship skills such as understanding other's perspectives, reading nonverbal cues, and making concessions (Siegel, 2012). These issues can be especially challenging for students from different cultures. Unfortunately, conflicts are difficult to explain away and are likely to occur due to a lack of understanding of the new country's culture.

Teaching culture has always been essential in world language classrooms. Initially, high culture, literature, and the arts, were taught. The teaching of high culture is no longer relevant to the real everyday experiences that students now face (Scarino, 2010).

Intercultural capability is the ability to interpret, create, and exchange meaning through communication among and across people. Intercultural capability is a student's ability to value their own cultures, languages, and beliefs, as well as those of others. Students may learn about diverse cultures in ways where they can recognize both similarities and differences, create connections with others, and foster mutual respect.

A teaching culture is always important with world language learning, which extends beyond developing cultural awareness to an intercultural capability. The goals of language learning extend beyond developing cultural awareness to intercultural capability.

Reciprocal interpretation and the meaning-making process occur across languages and cultures (Scarino, 2010). Students learn to analyze processes better while improving their language ability. They also learn how to interpret and understand human communication in new ways.

Interculturality involves the engagement of interpreting the interculturality in others. Language and culture are integral to the experience of learning because learners depend on language. Language is more than a containment of knowledge: it is an expression of it.

When students communicate in speaking and writing in the target language, students negotiate meaning through interpreting and using language in diverse contexts (Scarino, 2010). At the same time, they interact with others through diverse social, linguistic, and cultural worldviews and vocabulary.

In the world language classroom, the focus is on how students negotiate meaning in interactions. Students must learn how to manage the variability demanded by the particular context of communication such as formal and informal speech (Scarino, 2010). Students learn how to exchange meaning in language through analyzing, explaining, collaborating, and elaborating.

Language helps society maintain relationships while presenting and performing our own identities and roles. Our language shapes our thoughts and how we can communicate effectively. Motivated world language students have the ability to develop a worldview, unlike their monolingual peers.

These students demonstrate greater creativity and adaptability because of their tolerance.

All cultures address the teaching of **SEL** differently. Nonetheless, brain breaks are a necessity for most cultures in some form to promote positive learning. It is important to recognize that conflict is all right and that there will be differences to explain for multiple cultures.

QUESTIONS FOR EDUCATORS

1. How can teachers effectively teach culture?
2. How can teachers celebrate the differences of cultures in the classroom?
3. How can **SEL** and culture be used together to reach more students?

QUESTIONS FOR SCHOOL LEADERS

1. When conducting classroom observations, what does positive culture look like?
2. How can **SEL** improve a school's culture?
3. How can schools work to bridge differences between family and schools regarding **SEL** and culture practices?

ADDITIONAL RESOURCE

The Whole-Brain Child

Daniel Siegel's book provides a neuropsychiatrist's approach to raising children with strategies to encourage healthy brain development (Siegel, 2012). Although the book is written for parents, it provides a helpful model for educators in that it suggests effective strategies to facilitate long-term developmental learning. The book explains why children have conflicts and what the adult authority figure can do to address those conflicts which occur quite frequently in the education space.

Atkinson. (2002). Toward a sociocognitive approach to second language acquisition. *The Modern Language Journal, 86*(4), 525–545.

Duckworth. (2016). *Grit: The power of passion and perseverance.* New York, NY: Scribner.

Garcia. (1993). Language, culture, and education. *Review of Research in Education, 29,* 51–98.

Goleman. (2005). *Emotional intelligence.* New York, NY: Bantam Books.

Hoffman. (2009). Reflecting on social emotional learning: A critical perspective on trends in the United States. *Review of Educational Research, 79*(2), 533–556.

Lazear. (1999). Culture and language. *Journal of Political Economy, 107*(S6), S95–S126. doi:10.1086/250105.

Newmeyer. (1987). The current convergence in linguistic theory: Some implications for second language acquisition research. *Second Language Research, 3*(1), 1–19.

Sarles. (1976). On the problem: The origin of language. *Sign Language Studies, 11,* 149–182.

Scarino. (2010). Assessing intercultural capability in learning languages: A renewed understanding of language, culture, learning, and the nature of assessment. *The Modern Language Journal, 94*(2), 324–329.

Scott, Dessein, Ledford, & Joseph-Gabriel. (2013). Language awareness in the French classroom. *The French Review, 86,* 1160–1172.

Siegel. (2012). *The whole brain child.* New York: Random House.

Tochon. (2009). The key to global understanding: World languages education—Why schools need to adapt. *Review of Educational Research, 79*(2), 650–681.

US Census Bureau. (2015). Detailed languages spoken at home and ability to speak English for the population 5 years and over: 2009–2013. Retrieved from https://www.census.gov/data/tables/2013/demo/2009-2013-lang-tables.html.

Chapter 10

SEL and Distance Learning

During the COVID-19 pandemic crisis, the need for **SEL** during the distance learning process became quickly apparent. Many students are experiencing stress during this crisis due to sick family members, unemployed parents, and the need to work as essential workers themselves. More than ever, both teachers and students need **SEL** to stay calm, complete work and assignments, and relieve stress. A discussion of **SEL** resources and personal experiences illuminate problems and solutions for teachers and students during the COVID-19 crisis.

SEL DISTANCE LEARNING RESOURCES

There have been many resources from the Yale Center for Emotional Intelligence, CASEL, PanoramaEd, and Education Week, just to name a few. Even **SEL** programs such as Second Step, which is a K-8 program, have provided Zoom lessons for school districts. While read-alouds and singing have been beneficial for young children, connections and real conversations have been beneficial for older students. Many organizations are promoting this kind of **SEL** outreach such as the Committee for Children, a global nonprofit whose mission is to promote the safety and well-being of children through **SEL** in a peaceful world.

The focus of the Second Step and the Committee for Children is for the adults to model trust-building relationships and ownership. Students improve their relationships with their peers, their families, and other adults when they have positive relationships with trust. Families start to perceive their **high school** children more as adults and trust them with more information.

There are many resources available online to meet students' **SEL** needs. For instance, an effective educational tool called BrainPop has been providing free resources. BrainPop consists of educational websites with over 1,000 short animated movies for students in grades K-12. There are quizzes and related materials which cover science, social studies, English, math, technology, health, and arts and music.

There are effective resources from the Yale Center for educational Intelligence/RULER. Greater Good in Education offers free **SEL** activities and practices. CASEL has additional resources on **SEL** and COVID-19 for educators and parents. These and other resources are available in the site mentioned in the additional resource section of this chapter.

PERSONAL EXPERIENCE WITH DISTANCE LEARNING AND THE NEED FOR SEL

From personal experience, it is evident that there is an equity issue with distance learning. Many students do not have access to technology. Over 400 students at my school obtained a Google Chromebook laptop when our schools temporarily closed. Yet, some parents work too many jobs to have time to pick one up. Although my school district professionally developed teachers to use Zoom or Google Meet for live classes, Zoom does not function on a Chromebook. That is an equity issue if students are provided the technology that does not support the software used to deliver virtual classes.

Furthermore, there were technological issues with students accessing the online textbook either due to log-in issues, clearing internet browser cache issues, or because the textbook manufacturer app mysteriously disappeared twice for hours on two separate days. Students were constantly sending emails or sending private Google Classroom comments that they could not access the book. The school district's online systems were not equipped for this much student usage.

The school district requires teachers to contact parents when they are not submitting online assignments or are not virtually attending class. This process became an issue when students were actually getting COVID-19 themselves and could not submit work due to illness or were in the process of getting tested at testing sites. IEP meetings were canceled because family members were ill with COVID-19. Students were working in grocery stores making supplemental income for their parents who had lost their jobs. These students could not attend virtual classes, yet teachers were required to reach out to parents to inform them of their child's nonparticipation.

Internally, online Zoom meetings for departments were conducted more than school-wide check-in meetings. More department meetings occurred while out of school than in school. Yet, there were chances to actually ask questions to administration directly which does not exist while teachers and students are in school. More teacher collaboration within departments occurred with schools closed than open.

There were plenty of professional development opportunities offered by the school, the county, the textbook manufacturer, the College Board, and other educational entities. The amount of professional development trainings was daunting. They were also usually available in the evenings, which made it even more difficult to find a work-life balance. Participation is made even more difficult when teachers have their own children.

There were many online resources to use such as Pear Deck and Screencastify. Pear Deck is an interactive tool for presentations to use with such virtual meeting platforms as Zoom and Google Meet. Students can have their phones out and feel that they have a voice in the virtual classroom by responding to prompts from the teachers either requiring them to draw or to respond. Screencastify is another resource to create short video lessons.

The county provided professional development trainings in Google Classroom for novices and advanced users. There were many teachers who do not normally use Google Classroom for their students. This was the easiest method to learn for students to be able to submit their work without overwhelming a teacher's inbox. If a teacher did not already have Google Classroom set up, this process would be extremely overwhelming.

Other professional development included Zoom, Google Meet, and Screencastify. Teachers could use either Zoom or Google Meet. Zoom has more advanced options such as changing backgrounds and using breakout rooms for students. Google Meet is more equitable though for school districts that use Google Chromebooks for their students without access to technology. Teachers made their decisions based on their instructional needs and the needs of their students.

To address challenges in reaching students during this time, I asked them to do reflections of what they were doing while schools were closed and how they were preparing for the AP exam. I asked them to discuss their strengths and weaknesses and what they needed to study more for the AP exam. The students were very open about their reflections. They shared that they were working, babysitting, playing videogames, catching up with friends through FaceTime, TikTok, and Fortnite. We also discussed these reflections during our virtual classes which we could only hold once a week on a Friday.

I pre-recorded my level 1 classes and posted them in advance in Google Classroom. When students had comprehension questions regarding the work, I would ask them if they had watched the lesson video. When the online textbook did not function, I would ask students to pause on the lesson video. During this time, many simple solutions had to be created to meet student needs. Students asked questions at all times of day and night, weekends, and otherwise. It was difficult to have a work-life balance, making the **SEL** needs for educators all the more important.

The Yale Center for Emotional Intelligence and CASEL conducted a survey of more than 5,000 teachers in late March 2020 and found them to be overwhelmed, anxious, and stressed. The five most-mentioned feelings among all teachers were: anxious, fearful, worried, overwhelmed, and sad (Cipriano & Brackett, 2020). Anxiety was the most frequently mentioned emotion. Unfortunately, most teachers do not receive an education in emotions, making this crisis especially difficult to manage.

I participated in this survey, and I must say that I was dealing with the effects of the health and economic crisis within my school's community and my own family. The greatest finding from the survey is that we need a greater focus on teachers' health and well-being now, so they can thrive through this pandemic and be ready to return to school after this crisis has finished (Cipriano & Brackett, 2020).

These challenging events make **SEL** all the more important and needed for myself and my students. I did not want to burden my students with my own concerns during this time which made me have to practice my own emotional regulation. I endeavored to show compassion to my students, so that they could sense at least one educator cared what was happening to them during this crisis.

Students and teachers both need the **SEL** tools to manage stress and their emotions during these challenging times. Without effective emotional regulation, the anxiety of family members potentially contracting the disease, their physical sickness from the disease, and potential job losses will inevitably affect students, their families, and teachers. The ability to come back from these challenges with resilience and positivity is the only way that schools and communities can overcome this unexpected adversity.

QUESTIONS FOR TEACHERS

1. How can teachers professionally develop themselves to deliver effective instruction online simultaneously using **SEL** for their students?
2. How do teachers conduct norming for students they met in person all year long and then all of a sudden need to teach online?
3. How do teachers determine the most effective online tools to meet their virtual instructional needs?

QUESTIONS FOR SCHOOL LEADERS

1. How can schools address problems with equity and distance learning such as access to technology, sick family members, and the need for students to work while addressing their **SEL** needs?
2. How can schools become more flexible in responding to student's distance learning needs using **SEL**?
3. How can school leaders support teachers' and families' **SEL** needs online?

ADDITIONAL RESOURCE

SEL and Self-Care Resources for Educators, Schools, and Parents Related to COVID-19

There are many useful **SEL** resources on this site. For example, Common-Sense Media has provided lists of documentaries, films, apps, and other recommended resources. There are **SEL** apps for students to stay focused,

SEL distance learning reflection and planning toolkits, and trauma-informed **SEL** strategies (Woolf, 2020).

Cipriano, & Brackett. (2020). Teachers are anxious and overwhelmed. They need SEL now more than ever. Retrieved from https://www.edsurge.com/news/2020-0 4-07-teachers-are-anxious-and-overwhelmed-they-need-sel-now-more-than-ever.

Woolf. (2020). SEL and self-care resources for educators, schools, and parents related to COVID-19. Retrieved from https://www.panoramaed.com/blog/sel-resources-for-educators-school-communities-and-parents-related-to-covid-19.

References

ASCD. (2011). A whole child approach to education and the Common Core State Standards Initiative. Retrieved from http://www.ascd.org/ASCD/pdf/siteASCD/policy/CCSS-and-Whole-Child-one-pager.pdf.

Atkinson. (2002). Toward a sociocognitive approach to second language acquisition. *The Modern Language Journal, 86*(4), 525–545.

Bandura. (1997). *Self-efficacy: The exercise of control*. New York, NY: Freeman.

Bandura. (2001). Social cognitive theory: An agentic perspective. *Annual Review of Psychology, 52*, 1–26. (Siegel, 2012).

Barth. (1990). *Improving schools from within: Teachers, parents, and principals can make the difference*. San Francisco: Jossey-Bass.

Bartolino Krachman, Arnold, & Larocca. (2016). *Expanding the definition of student success: A case study of the CORE districts*. Retrieved from Boston, MA: http://www.transformingeducation.org/core-toolkit/.

Bear. (2010). *School discipline and self-discipline: A practical guide to promoting prosocial student behavior*. New York: The Guilford Press.

Berryhill, Linney, & Fromewick. (2009). The effects of education accountability on teachers: Are policies too-stress provoking for their own good? *International Journal of Education Policy and Leadership, 4*(5), 1–14.

Bird, & Sultmann. (2010). Social and emotional learning: Reporting a system approach to developing relationships, nurturing well-being and invigorating learning. *Educational & Child Psychology, 27*(1), 143–155.

Blackwell, Trzesniewski, & Dweck. (2007). Implicit theories of intelligence predict achievement across an adolescent transition: A longitudinal study and an intervention. *Child Development, 78*(1), 246–263.

Bookman, N. (2015, December 7). Personal interview.

Bracey. (1998). An optimal size for high schools? *Phi Delta Kappan, 79*(5), 406.

Bracey. (2005). The 15th Bracey report on the condition of public education. *Phi Delta Kappan, 87,* 138–153.

Brackett. (2019). *Permission to feel: Unlocking the power of emotions to help our kids, ourselves, and our society thrive.* New York: NY: Celadon Books.

Carroll, & Carroll. (2002). *Statistics made simple for school leaders. Data-driven decision making.* Lanham, MD: Scarecrow Education.

CASEL. (2003). Safe and sound: An educational leader's guide to evidence-based social and emotional learning (SEL) programs. Retrieved from http://indiana.edu/~pbisin/pdf/Safe_and_Sound.pdf.

CASEL. (2012). 2013 CASEL guide: Effective social and emotional learning programs—Preschool and elementary school edition. Retrieved from http://www.casel.org/library/2013-casel-guide.

CASEL. (2013). CASEL's collaborating districts initiative (CDI). Retrieved from http://www.casel.org/collaborating-districts/.

CASEL. (2017). What is SEL. Retrieved from http://www.casel.org/what-is-sel/.

Clark, & Clark. (2004). Principal leadership for developing and sustaining highly successful middle level schools. *Middle School Journal, 36*(2), 49–55.

Clark, & Clark. (2006). Middle school leadership: What should accountability really mean to school leaders? *Middle School Journal, 37*(4), 52–58.

Conley. (2007). *Toward a more comprehensive conception of college readiness.* Eugene, OR: Educational Policy Improvement Center.

CORE. (2016). The school quality improvement index & the CORE data collaborative. Retrieved from http://coredistricts.org/wp-content/uploads/2016/01/CORE-Data-Collaborative-v3-1-21-16.pdf.

Cuban. (1998). How schools change reforms: Redefining reform success and failure. *Teachers College Record, 99,* 453–477.

Darling-Hammond, Wilhoit, & Pittenger. (2014). Accountability for college and career readiness: Developing a new paradigm. *Education Policy Analysis Archives, 22,* 86.

DePaoli, Atwell, & Bridgeland. (2017). *Ready to lead: A national principal survey on how social and emotional learning can prepare children and transform schools: A report for CASEL.* Retrieved from Washington, DC.

Duckworth. (2016). *Grit: The power of passion and perseverance.* New York, NY: Scribner.

Duckworth, Quinn, & Tsukayama. (2012). What No Child Left Behind leaves behind: The roles of IQ and self-control in predicting standardized achievement test scores and report card 29 grades. *Journal of Educational Psychology, 104*(2), 439–451.

Duckworth, & Seligman. (2005). Self-discipline out-does IQ in predicting academic performance of adolescents. *Psychological Science, 16*(12), 939–944.

Duckworth, & Yeager. (2015). Measurement matters: Assessing personal qualities other than cognitive ability for educational purposes. *Educational Researcher, 44*(4), 237–251.

Dweck. (2006). *Mindset: The new psychology of success.* New York: Random House.

ED. (2016). *Every student succeeds act: Accountability, state plans, and data reporting: Summary of final regulations.* Washington, DC: U.S. Department of Education.

Ee, Mingming, & Wong. (2014). Teachers' infusion of social emotional learning. *Journal of Teaching and Teacher Education, 2*(1), 27–45.

Egley. (2005). Principals' inviting leadership behaviors in a time of test-based accountability. *Scholar-Practitioner Quarterly, 3*(1), 13–24.

Eid, & Diener. (2006). Introduction: The need for multimethod measurement in psychology. In *American Psychological Association handbook of multimethod measurement in psychology* (pp. 3–8). Washington, DC: American Psychological Association.

Elias. (2004). The connection between social-emotional learning and learning disabilities: Implications for intervention. *Learning Disability Quarterly, 27*(1), 53–63. doi:10.2307/1593632.

Elias, Zins, Weissberg, Frey, Greenberg, Haynes, & Schriver. (1997). *Promoting social and emotional learning: Guidelines for Educators.* Alexandria, VA: ASCD.

Farkas. (2003). Cognitive skills and noncognitive traits and behaviors in stratification process. *Annual Review of Psychology, 29,* 541–562.

Farrington, Roderick, Allensworth, Nagaoka, Keyes, Johnson, & Beechum. (2012). *Teaching adolescents to become learners: The role of noncognitive factors in shaping school performance—A critical literature review* (978-0-9856-8190-6). Retrieved from http://proxygw.wrlc.org/login?url=http://search.ebscohost.com/login.aspx?direct=true&db=eric&AN=ED542543&site=ehost-live.

Fredricks, Blumenfeld, & Paris. (2004). School engagement: Potential of the concept, state of the evidence. *Review of Educational Research, 74*(1), 59–109.

Friedman, Kern, Hampson, & Duckworth. (2014). A new lifespan approach to conscientiousness and health: Combining the pieces of the causal puzzle. *Development and Psychology, 50*(5), 1377–1389.

Garcia. (1993). Language, culture, and education. *Review of Research in Education, 29,* 51–98.

Goldwyn. (2007). School leadership that works: From research to results. *Journal of Educational Administration, 45*(3), 340–342.

Goleman. (2005). *Emotional intelligence.* New York, NY: Bantam Books.

Goleman, Boyatzis, & McKee. (2002). *Primal leadership: Realizing the power of emotional intelligence.* Boston: Harvard Business School Press.

Hagger, Wood, Stiff, & Chatzisarantis. (2010). Ego depletion and the strength model of self-control: A meta-analysis. *Psychological Bulletin, 136*(4), 495–525.

Hammond. (2015). *Culturally responsive teaching and the brain: Promoting authentic engagement and rigor among culturally and linguistically diverse students.* Thousand Oaks, CA: Corwin.

Heckman, & Rubinstein. (2001). *The importance of noncognitive skills: Lessons from GED testing program.* Paper presented at the American Economic Review.

Heckman, Strixrud, & Urzua. (2006). The effects of cognitive and noncognitive abilities on labor market outcomes and social behavior. *Journal of Labor Economics, 24*(3), 411–482. doi:10.3386/w12006.

Hoffman. (2009). Reflecting on social emotional learning: A critical perspective on trends in the United States. *Review of Educational Research, 79*(2), 533–556.

Honig, & Coburn. (2008). Evidence-based decision making in school district central offices: Toward a policy and research agenda. *Educational Policy, 22*(4), 578–608.

Inlay. (2016). Creating a culture of respect through the implicit curriculum. *Middle School Journal, 47*(2), 23–31.

Ireland, & Pennebaker. (2010). Language style matching in writing: Synchrony in essays, correspondence, and poetry. *Journal of Personality and Social Psychology, 99*, 549–571.

Jackson, & Lunenburg. (2010). School performance indicators, accountability ratings, and student achievement. *American Secondary Education, 39*(1), 27–44.

Jacob. (2002). Where the boys aren't: Non-cognitive skills, returns to school and the gender gap in higher education. *Economics of Education Review, 21*(6), 589–598.

Jennings. (2010). School choice or schools' choice? Managing in an era of accountability. *Sociology of Education, 83*(3), 227–247.

Jones. (2005). The myths of data-driven schools. *Principal Leadership, 6*(2), 37–39.

Jones, Bailey, & Jacob. (2014). Social-emotional learning is essential to classroom management. *The Phi Delta Kappan, 96*(2), 19–24.

Jones, Bouffard, & Weissbour. (2013). Educators' social and emotional skills vital to learning. *The Phi Delta Kappan, 94*(8), 62–65.

Jones, Jones, & Vermette. (2009). Using social and emotional learning to foster academic achievement in secondary mathematics. *American Secondary Education, 37*(3), 4–9.

Kidd, Palmeri, & Aslin. (2013). Rational snacking: Young children's decision-making on the marshmallow task is moderated by beliefs about environmental reliability. *Cognition, 126*(1), 109–114.

Kress, Norris, Schoenholz, Elias, & Seigle. (2004). Bringing together educational standards and social and emotional learning: Making the case for educators. *American Journal of Education, 111*(1), 68–89. doi:10.1086/424720.

Kyllonen. (2012). The importance of higher education and the role of non cognitive attributes in college success. *Revista de Investigación Educacional Latinoamericana, 49*(2), 84–100.

Lazear. (1999). Culture and language. *Journal of Political Economy, 107*(S6), S95–S126. doi:10.1086/250105.

Lee, Lee, & Jang. (2015). How important are non-cognitive personality and personal background to the unemployment persistence in Korea? *Korea and the World Economy, 16*(3), 345–377. Retrieved from http://www.akes.or.kr/akes/eng/publication/publication_07.asp?data_where=3.

Lewis. (2004). *Employee perspectives on implementation communication as predictors of perceptions of success and resistance.* University of Texas at Austin, Unpublished manuscript.

Lindahl. (2012). A study of school size among Alabama's public high schools. *International Journal of Education Policy and Leadership, 7*(1), 1–27.

Loeb, & Figlio (Eds.). (2011). *School accountability* (Vol. 3). San Diego, CA: North Holland.

Lombardi, Seburn, & Conley. (2011). Development and initial validation of a measure of academic behaviors associated with college and career readiness. *Journal of Career Assessment, 19*(4), 375–391.

Longshore. (2016). Play your cards right. *Principal Leadership, 16*(8), 53–55.

Lopes, Mestre, Guil, Kremenitzer, & Salovey. (2012). The role of knowledge and skills for managing emotions in adaption to school: Social behavior and misconduct in the classroom. *American Educational Research Journal, 49*(4), 710–742.

Lyons. (2004). The influence of socioeconomic factors on Kentucky's public school accountability system: Does poverty impact school effectiveness? *Education Policy Analysis Archives, 12*, 37.

Lyons, & Algozzine. (2006). Perceptions of the impact of accountability on the role of principals. *Education Policy Analysis Archives, 14*(16), 1–19.

Melnick, Cook-Harvey, & Darling-Hammond. (2017). *Encouraging social and emotional learning in the context of new accountability.* Palo Alto, CA: Learning Policy Institute.

Melnick, & Martinez. (2019). *Preparing teachers to support social and emotional learning: A case study of San Jose University and Lakewood Elementary School.* San Palto, CA: Learning Policy Institute.

Nagaoka, Farrington, Ehrlich, & Heath. (2015). *Foundations for young adult success: A developmental framework*. Retrieved from Chicago, IL: https://consortium.uchicago.edu/sites/default/files/publications/Wallace%20Report.pdf.

Newmeyer. (1987). The current convergence in linguistic theory: Some implications for second language acquisition research. *Second Language Research, 3*(1), 1–19.

NHDOE. (u.d.). New Hampshire accountability pilot overview: Performance assessment of competency education (PACE).

Ordu, & Ordu. (2012, Fall 2012). Seven levels of accountability for student success. *Source*. Retrieved from http://www.advanc-ed.org/source/seven-levels-accountability-student-success.

Page, C. (2020, February 10). Personal interview.

Paris, & Winograd (Eds.). (1990). *How metacognition can promote academic learning and instruction*. Hillsdale, NJ: Lawrence Erlbaum Associates.

Parke. (2012). Making use of district and school data. *Practical Assessment, Research & Evaluation, 17*(1), 10. Paunesku, Walton, Romero, Smith, Yeager, & Dweck. (2015). Mindset interventions are a scalable treatment for academic underachievement. *Psychological Science, 26*(6), 784–793.

Pearson. (2016). *Measurement of student level skills: The Virginia 5 Cs*. Arlington, VA: CNA.

Pittman, & Haughwout. (1987). Influence of high school size on dropout rate. *Education Evaluation and Policy Analysis, 9*(4), 337–343.

Putnam. (2015). *Our kids: The American dream in crisis*. New York: Simon & Schuster Paperbacks.

Ransford. (2007). *The role of school and teacher characteristics on teacher burnout and implementation quality of social-emotional learning curriculum*. Pennsylvania State University, Unpublished manuscript.

Rosen, Glennie, Dalton, Lennon, & Bozick. (2010). No cognitive skills in the classroom: New perspectives on educational research. *RTI Press publication No. BK-0004-1009*.

Rothstein. (2014). *Accountability for noncognitive skills*. Alexandria, VA: AASA.

Rushton, Brainerd, & Pressley. (1983). Behavioral development and construct validity: The principle of aggregation. *Psychological Bulletin, 94*(1), 18.

Sarles. (1976). On the problem: The origin of language. *Sign Language Studies, 11*, 149–182.

Scarino. (2010). Assessing intercultural capability in learning languages: A renewed understanding of language, culture, learning, and the nature of assessment. *The Modern Language Journal, 94*(2), 324–329.

Schmidt, & Datnow. (2005). Teachers' sense-making about comprehensive school reform: The influence of emotions. *Teaching and Teacher Education, 21*(8), 949–965.

Schmoker. (2008). Measuring what matters. *Educational Leadership*, *66*(4), 70–74.
Schonert-Reichl. (2017). Social and emotional learning and teachers. *The Future of Children*, *27*(1), 137–155.
Scott, Dessein, Ledford, & Joseph-Gabriel. (2013). Language awareness in the French classroom. *The French Review*, *86*, 1160–1172.
Siegel. (2012). *The whole-brain child*. New York: Random House.
Spricks. (2020). About safe & civil schools. Retrieved from http://www.safeandcivilschools.com/aboutus/index.php.
Steinberg. (2014). What's holding back American teenagers? *Slate*. Retrieved from http://www.slate.com.
Szczesiul, Nehring, & Carey. (2015). Academic task demand in the 21st-century, high-stakes-accountability school: Mapping the journey from poor to excellent? *Leadership and Policy in Schools*, *14*(4), 460–489.
Tanner. (2014). *The impact of No Child Left behind on non-cognitive skills*. Retrieved from https://sites.google.com/site/patrickseantanner/job-market-paper.
Tochon. (2009). The key to global understanding: World languages education—Why schools need to adapt. *Review of Educational Research*, *79*(2), 650–681.
Tough. (2012). *How children succeed: Grit, curiosity, and the hidden power of character*. Boston, MA: Mariner Books and Houghton Mifflin Harcourt.
Ujifusa. (2016). Fact check: Does ESSA really require 'non-academic' accountability measures? *Education Week*. Retrieved from http://blogs.edweek.org/edweek/campaign-k-12/2016/03/fact_check_essa_non-academic.html.
US Census Bureau. (2015). Detailed languages spoken at home and ability to speak English for the population 5 years and over: 2009–2013. Retrieved from https://www.census.gov/data/tables/2013/demo/2009-2013-lang-tables.html.
Uskali. (2004). What are schools to watch? Retrieved from http://www.schoolstowatch.org/what.htm.
Valentine, Clark, Hackmann, & Petzko. (2004). *Leadership for highly successful middle level schools: Vol. II. A national study of leadership in middle level schools*. Reston, VA: National Association of Secondary School Principals.
Wahlstrom, Louis, Leithwood, & Anderson. (2010). *Investigating the links to improved student learning: Executive summary of research findings*. University of Minnesota: The Wallace Foundation.
West, Kraft, Finn, Martin, Duckworth, Gabrieli, & Gabrieli. (2014). Promise and paradox: Measuring students' non-cognitive skills and the impact of schooling. Retrieved from http://cepr.harvard.edu/files/cepr/files/cepr-promise-paradox.pdf.

Index

accountability, 1–20, 22, 53–57, 60–64, 66–68, 73, 76–80, 83–87, 90; Every Student Succeeds Act (ESSA), 2, 3, 4, 7, 8, 74, 86, 94; No Child Left Behind (NCLB), 1, 2, 4, 53, 57, 64, 84

assessment(s), 1–20, 54–61, 65–67, 76, 79, 84, 93, 103; reference bias, 6, 29, 55

Collaborative for Academic, Social, and Emotional Learning (CASEL), 3, 6, 9–11, 13, 14, 24, 57, 85, 95, 135, 136, 138

collective teacher efficacy (CTE), 92

college- and career-ready (CCR), 4, 38, 44

culturally responsive teaching (CRT), 93, 118; interculturality, 122

emotional intelligence, 3, 9, 10, 11, 19, 37, 39, 45, 47, 48, 74, 75, 101; metamood, 75; mindset(s), 5, 9, 10, 11, 13, 19, 20, 24, 31, 39, 49, 53, 59, 95, 97; noncognitive, 18, 19, 20, 31, 65; regulation, 11, 18, 66, 81, 102, 104, 107, 126, 138, 139

National Governor's Association (NGA), 1, 18

Positive Behavioral Interventions and Supports (PBIS), 28, 77, 88–90, 99, 108

social-emotional learning (SEL), 1–14, 17–32, 35–49, 53–68, 73–80, 83–99, 101–11, 113–32, 135–39; Recognizing, Understanding, Labeling, Expressing and Regulating (RULER), 102, 136; relationship skills, 3, 19, 20, 42, 43, 96, 126, 127, 128, 130; responsible decision-making, 3, 19, 20, 42, 45, 47, 96, 121, 125, 126; self-efficacy, 5, 10, 20, 39, 65, 75, 125, 129; self-management, 3, 10, 11, 13, 19, 20, 37, 39, 45, 47, 58, 65, 84, 96, 97, 125, 126; social awareness, 3, 10, 11, 19, 20, 41, 43, 45, 58, 96, 119, 121, 125, 126, 127, 130; social skills, 5, 11, 12, 13, 20, 37, 44, 45, 58, 59, 67

standard(s), 2, 5–16, 35–40, 42–50, 54, 55, 65

University of Chicago Consortium on School Research (CCSR), 3, 5, 13, 20

About the Author

Dr. Renee Carr, EdD, has been working in the field of education since 2007. Dr. Carr has a history of working in international and domestic education and exchange. She is multilingual and speaks Modern Greek, French, and Spanish. Dr. Carr has taught English abroad through the Teaching Assistant Program in France-United States. She has worked at a university, nonprofits, and two school districts in the Washington, DC, area, such as Family Health International (FHI) 360, the College Board, American University, Fairfax County Public Schools, and Prince George's County Public Schools. She obtained her doctorate in Educational Administration and Policy Studies from the George Washington University in May 2019. The premise of this book came from her dissertation topic, and she added her own experiences as an educator both from the perspectives of world language education and the COVID-19 crisis.

www.ingramcontent.com/pod-product-compliance
Lightning Source LLC
Chambersburg PA
CBHW020740230426
43665CB00009B/505